BLACK COMMUNITIES
of FAIRFAX

BLACK COMMUNITIES
of **FAIRFAX**

A History

Etta Willson, Rita Colbert,
Linneall Naylor, Rondia Prescott
with Jenee Lindner

THE
History
PRESS

Published by The History Press
Charleston, SC
www.historypress.com

Front cover, top left: Mount Calvary Baptist Church. *Courtesy of Rita Colbert. Top center*: Black Fairfax, Virginia jury, 1935. *Courtesy of the Virginia Room, Fairfax County Public Library. Top right*: Willie Mulkey riding his bike in the School Street neighborhood. *Courtesy of Rita Colbert. Bottom*: Fairfax Rosenwald School. *Used with permission from Fisk University, John Hope and Aurelia E. Franklin Library, Julius Rosenwald Archives, Special Collections, Nashville, Tennessee.*
Back cover: Aerial map of Fairfax City, Virginia, 1957. *Courtesy of the Virginia Room, Fairfax County Public Library.*

First published 2024
Updated printing 2024

Manufactured in the United States

ISBN 9781467155496

Library of Congress Control Number: 2023945806

For our families and our extraordinary ancestors

CONTENTS

Part II. Segregated Communities in Fairfax, Virginia

Part III. Making a Difference

FOREWORD

The history of Black communities in our country has gone largely unwritten for centuries. Much has been lost, and yet an astonishing amount has been preserved. Photos, letters, news articles and oral histories have been preserved and passed down from one generation to the next. The journey to discover a more robust history of the city we live in has been undertaken by a new generation eager to make certain a larger understanding of Black heritage is uncovered and passed on.

Years ago, we could not have guessed what mysteries would be unlocked by readily available DNA testing. We couldn't have guessed even twenty years ago how email, the Internet and online platforms like Ancestry.com and Facebook would change how we connect with one another, through the ability to share photos digitally, to look up census information online, to track down property histories, to put out a call for help in finding information.

This book is about how all these innovations, connections and people came together to shape an important story about the Black community as it existed in Fairfax City. The families that lived here, both Black and White, going back to the nineteenth century, are far more intertwined than we previously understood.

I am grateful to the many contributors who made this important work of scholarship possible. It is a Fairfax City treasure that will live on for generations to tell the important story of how our Black communities left their imprint on our history.

Catherine S. Read
Mayor, City of Fairfax, Virginia
July 2023

PREFACE

One generation will commend your works to another; They will tell of your mighty acts. They will speak of the glorious splendor of your majesty. And I will meditate on your wonderful works. They will tell of the power of your awesome works, and I will proclaim your great deeds. They will celebrate your abundant goodness and joyfully sing of your righteousness.
—Psalms 145:4–7

This scripture represents the older generation sharing memories that will edify and inspire the next generation. Memories we cherish are links in the chain that connect us to the past and serve as a bridge to the future. I am honored to share the memories of my family and community and to contribute to this special project.

My name is Etta (Allen) Willson. I was born in Fairfax, Virginia, in a segregated community located half a mile south of the old Fairfax Court House called the School Street community. My parents were Phillip Allen and Virginia Payne Allen. We lived on Route 123 (Chain Bridge Road) near East and West School Streets. It is today next to George Mason University. My parents purchased their property in 1930. I know the history of the area as well as the families and where they all lived. We were all connected biologically or by marriage. This is where I attended school, went to church and learned the moral value of strong family ties. I will always treasure the memories that I hold dear of cousins, aunts, uncles and friends who influenced my life.

Many of my ancestors also lived in the interracial Jermantown community of Fairfax, Virginia, about two miles northwest of School Street. They are buried there in the segregated Jermantown Cemetery. I remember attending the burial of my maternal grandfather, Reverend Benjamin Payne, at the cemetery. I chose to write an article about my grandfather because he was a well-respected minister of the Gospel, esteemed both by family and the community. His reputation was beyond reproach.

It is rewarding to know that the story of these historic neighborhoods will, at last, be shared. I am so proud to be a part of it.

Etta Willson
Descendant of the Payne and Allen families
January 2023

This book began as an article about the African American Jermantown Cemetery in Fairfax, Virginia, and its founding in 1868. Then it expanded, as descendants wrote the initial histories of ancestors buried there. The authors are Etta Willson, Rita Colbert, Linneall Naylor, Rondia Prescott and Jenee Lindner. We all are daughters, wives and mothers. It became clear as we looked at our common family roots that we found ourselves on this valuable memory lane together. We would stop, look and then move forward up this ancestral path of lives lived. We realized we had a lot more to tell readers at our fingertips. A book was born.

We begin with the history of Jermantown Cemetery, including a cemetery survey list of those we know are buried there. There may be more. There is no official list in existence that was kept, we believe. We discuss the cemetery's history and the people who were cemetery trustees, nonprofit organizations from yesterday to today, commemorations, and cleanup crews from several religious organizations. But, most importantly, we discuss cemetery ancestors through neighborhood friendships and family research, done by their descendants.

We share stories from personal memories. All the book's authors are related somehow by blood or marriage. For some of us, having been raised as children with our families in Fairfax City in the segregated communities of Jermantown and School Street, it became important to talk about our old surroundings, too. For example, maps were made of the twentieth-century communities where we grew up that are no longer in existence. Information about the importance of church and education in our communities is highlighted. The descriptions of that time and the old pictures are wonderfully enriching.

To lay a foundation to discuss more in this book, I, Jenee, stepped back and researched the history of the Fairfax area before 1868 through the African American lens. My work included a deeper dive into familial roots, with the construction of the town and the Little River Turnpike. Both the town and the turnpike infrastructure were created by many of their ancestors. We decided to include writings from the George Mason University Center for Mason Legacies: Black Lives Next Door and excerpts from the well-researched Historic Fairfax City Inc. newsletters, to name a few. They all gave additional insight into the Black communities of Fairfax.

So, who are we?

Etta Willson has been the lead family genealogist for forty-three years and counting. Sadly, her husband died two years ago. She now resides with her daughter Leslie's family and grandchildren. She loves being with them. However, after some time, she decided to continue pursuing her passion for genealogical research. Etta has an extensive family collection going back many years. She was essential in helping create the cemetery burial list, since there is no longer an official list on record. She fondly remembers her early years of growing up in the School Street area, as well as the oral history she heard from relatives over the years. She worked on the community maps from memory with the help of Rita Colbert, Earl Marshall and others. She has records, newspaper clippings and information that was vital for this book's completion. She is a very good writer and a lovely friend. This could not have been done without her input, expertise and understanding. Etta really gets into the details. She introduced me to those I have been writing about at the recent Payne family reunion. I took pictures she suggested, which were most helpful. I met her sister Pauline Taylor (eighty-nine years young!), who is the wife of Reverend Booker Taylor, mentioned elsewhere in the book. I also met her classmates from the Fairfax Rosenwald School. Etta is smiling more.

Linneall Naylor is a special education instructional assistant for Fairfax County Public Schools. She has been there from the first July 2021 summer event I facilitated on behalf of a grassroots religious-based racial unity reconciliation group (RRG) that is made up of several different churches. Its mission is to erase discrimination and injustice with healing by "Gathering in Humility to Listen, Learn, and Serve." My task, which

I happily volunteered to do, was to help coordinate and connect with Jermantown Cemetery descendants and, hopefully, as a Fairfax historian and founder of my own nonprofits, to facilitate a new nonprofit for the Jermantown Cemetery. (Faith without works is dead.) We had meetings first at my house and then at Mount Calvary Baptist Church in Fairfax. The purpose of these early meetings was to share historical material in existence, generate interest and support the creation of a nonprofit organization that would document, preserve, protect, maintain and advocate for the Jermantown Cemetery. With nonprofit status, it could receive funds tax-free from donors to help meet these goals. Linneall was always there, starting at the first organization meeting. She was willing to do anything on behalf of her Jermantown Cemetery ancestors. After the meetings at my home concluded, Linneall led the organizational meetings at the church. Her leadership has never stopped since. She became the founding vice president of the Jermantown Cemetery Preservation Society nonprofit, created in October 2021. Today, she is the president. She knows the Ancestry.com technology on her phone very well, especially DNA connections, and can quickly access her research about her long line of families. She is very involved with many family associations, from Montpelier to family cemeteries in Fredericksburg to the recent Payne family reunion and the Liberia House in Manassas, Virginia, where her Naylor ancestors were enslaved by the Carter family. Linneall delights in doing genealogical work and praises the Lord when she finds new facts during her research. Her children have also been lovingly involved in this work, supporting her and her great efforts for a little heaven on earth, Linneall style! Linneall is a rock from which duties flow.

Rita Colbert has pictures of everybody! She even has the photo collection of a close relative who used to take pictures every Sunday, years ago, throughout their community. And, importantly, she remembers who the subjects are. This book is a rare opportunity for the public to see some of this private photo collection. When Rita saw a draft of this book, the first thing out of her mouth was, "My name is everywhere!" That is what happens when you are the community picture lady! She helped make the all-important maps by proofing and shepherding them, with my son, Sam, to completion. Newspaper clippings to share? Yep, she has them. She is a bright light. Rita takes care of her grandchildren during the day and loves talking about the old days in Jermantown and School Street. She has quite the network of kin who have become involved in Jermantown Cemetery's restoration, as well. They are all delightful and right there, always ready to support any Jermantown Cemetery efforts with lots of family interaction and participation. Rita is just someone you want to be around to enjoy.

Rondia Prescott is the youngest of all of us and niece to Rita. She is a Fairfax County (SACC) substitute staff supervisor/coordinator. Rondia has become a great crusader of learning and teaching about her ancestors. Her collection is proof of her expertise in nuanced family details and the fact that she loves ("adores" might be a better word!) family genealogy. She is vice president of the Jermantown Cemetery Preservation Society. At the 2022 Payne family reunion, she said in so many words, "Despite being enslaved, most not even given the opportunity to learn to read and write—yet, after they were freed, they bought land, raised large families and made opportunities for themselves and their posterity. I am in awe of their survival spirit. I am proud to be their descendant." Hear! Hear! I wholeheartedly agree. For the August 20, 2023 Jermantown Cemetery Legacy Day event, she made a twenty-panel, six-foot-high display sharing her research and love for her family and their communities. It was museum quality. It explained—with hundreds of individual photos, newspaper obituaries and other materials—Black lives in Fairfax, Virginia. Rondia's children were involved and have spoken positively about her passion on her behalf. She shows by motherly example to them the joy and importance of family genealogy work. They get it.

I, Jenee Lindner, am a longtime genealogist, as are Etta, Rita, Linneall and Rondia. I am also a Fairfax County history commissioner. For over thirty years, I have done research and given historical lectures, tours and living history reenactments about Fairfax City and Fairfax County. I have actively volunteered on several history boards, including those of Historic Fairfax City Inc. and the Fairfax Railroad Museum. I chaired the Fairfax City walking tours for ten years. I have given numerous local history tours beyond the city—for Fairfax County, George Mason University and the Virginia Museum of History and Culture, to name a few—through my work as founder and president of the Friends of the Historic Fairfax Courthouse. I am always on the lookout for the history of *all* the city's former residents. I have found it with descendants of Jermantown Cemetery and their Fairfax City formerly segregated communities who are willing to share. In 2022, I was chosen, to my great surprise, as one of a handful of that year's Fairfax County Community Champion Volunteers and Fairfax City Volunteers of the Year. My family has been key to my success, with their support and enthusiasm for this labor of love I do and for this calling I feel—especially, this time, my son, Sam, and my husband, Gary, on this book project. Sam was my armchair copyeditor, who also made all the maps we needed done. In addition, he was home (again when I hurt my back) and helped me by formatting it to the publisher's instructions after I collected the material from everyone involved and weaved it together. My husband went through the book and did the all-important index. Without Sam and Gary's expertise and technological support, it would have been difficult to achieve this miracle of a book.

In the summer of 2022, as part of the Payne family reunion weekend, a special church service was held on Sunday at the African American–founded Mount Calvary Baptist Church in Fairfax. Many of those buried at the Jermantown Cemetery worshipped there. Many of them built the church. The visiting Reverend Dr. Robert F. Cheeks said, "I am going to survive this." The congregation answered, "Me, too." He spoke further

> *Just as those before us, don't be victims; be survivalists. Accept, adjust, go on, advance despite your circumstances. Be a survivor in Christ! Have a survivor spirit, a survivor mentality. Remember these three letters: who and how. A victim is a who. He wallows in his trials. "Who has done this to me? Woe is me!" A survivalist is a how and moves forward. "How can I reach others to help me in this difficult circumstance—or I help them?" God will never close one door that He does not open another.*

This book is a history of survival and great accomplishments under societal hardship. Life is tough in any circumstances, but our ancestors had it tougher. By living their lives with love, dignity, hard work and faith in God and each other, they became like the leavening ingredient in bread. Their stories, person by person, family by family, street by street, can rise to show generations of wisdom and ways to thrive in the world for those who will stop, read and listen. We want people to know about our ancestors. We are grateful to join hands with them. This book is our offering to you.

One and God makes a majority.
—Frederick Douglass

Jenee Lindner, MA
March 2023

ACKNOWLEDGEMENTS

We would like to thank those who contributed to this book. First, our copyeditor and map designer, Sam Lindner. His technical writing skills and hours of formatting were paramount in getting armchair computer users like us to the goal line.

Thank you, director of the Virginia Room at the Fairfax County Public Libraries Christopher Barbuschak, for finding the additional maps and pictures we needed. It was quite a list. A special thank you to the Fairfax County Circuit Court Historical Records Center. Heather Bollinger, manager, plus Georgia Brown and Samantha Brice were extremely helpful.

A special thank you to all those who gave us permission to include their excellent articles: Brenda Duncan, Constance B. Smith, Ned Foster, Debbie Robison of Northern Virginia Notes (www.novahistory.org) William Page Johnson II of Historic Fairfax City Inc. (www.historicfairfax.org/history/ newsletter), Marion Dobbins, Anne Dobberteen, Dr. Robert Prichard, Michael Marrow, Jaya Patil, B.K. Morris, Frank Mustac and the George Mason University Center for Mason Legacies: Black Lives Next Door.

Thank you, Patrick O'Neill and, again, Sam Lindner, for helping with picture formats. Thank you, Gary Lindner, for doing this book's all-important index.

We would be remiss if we did not thank our acquisitions editor at Arcadia Publishing, Kate Jenkins. Your patience and expertise made all the difference.

Many helped in various ways. Thank you all. We are blessed.

INTRODUCTION

by Jenee Lindner

In the 1860 census, the total population of the state of Virginia (excluding West Virginia) was compiled as 1,239,725. The census listed 713,439 (57%) White residents and 526,286 (43%) Black. The Black census broke it down further to 468,244 (38%) enslaved and 58,042 (5%) free Black. There were more who were not counted because the freed enslaved often left Virginia for other states by crossing the Potomac River into Maryland. They were highly taxed in Virginia or forced back into servitude if they did not pay the local government regularly after gaining their freedom. This law incentivized them to leave once freed. Many did.[1]

Fairfax, Virginia, was originally called the Town of Providence (later nicknamed Fairfax Court House), in 1805. It was formally created a few years after Washington, D.C., in 1790. The locals like to call them twin towns/cities because the Fairfax County Courthouse was finished first, in 1800, for county-wide circuit court business. Washington, D.C., had its first U.S. congressional government session in 1800. The name was changed in 1874 to the Town of Fairfax and, finally, the City of Fairfax in 1961.[2] It is in the middle of Fairfax County and directly west of Washington, D.C. It was connected most prominently by the Little River Turnpike, a sixteen-mile day's walk point to point—or by horse, wagon or carriage, a little faster. Before the Civil War, many freedmen lived and worked locally in farming, animal husbandry, timber harvesting, sawmills, roadbuilding and blacksmithing. After the American Civil War in 1865, the town—then called Fairfax Court House—was nearly 30 percent African American.[3] In 1880, the proportion stayed about the same. Of the total population of 380 registered in the 1880 census, 125 were Black, almost one-third of the town.[4]

Below is a chart showing the population and partial demographics of Fairfax City, Virginia.

YEAR	POP.	White	Black	Asian	Hispanic	Multiracial	Other
1900	373						
1910	413						
1920	516						
1930	640						
1940	979						
1950	1,946	1,680	266				
1960	13,585	13,158	407	16			4
1970	21,970	21,509	370	64			27
1980	19,390	17,799	574	475	379		163
1990	19,622	16,100	936	1,372	1,159		55
2000	21,498	14,333	1,035	2,609	2,932	492	97
2010	22,565	13,849	1,030	3,403	3,556	606	121
2020	24,146	12,911	1,052	4,519	4,278	1,129	257

Fairfax County, Virginia, surrounding Fairfax City, is old by American standards. It was first a colonial British parish and was created in 1742, thirty-four years before the 1776 Declaration of Independence. Fairfax County's proximity to Washington, D.C., has become all-important for commerce and federal government employees living outside D.C. Therefore, it has become the most populous county in Virginia, with a total area of four hundred square miles today.

In 1860, Fairfax County was rural. It had a total population of only 11,834, including both White and Black residents. The White population was about 8,046 (68%) and the Black population 3,788 (32%). Of the Black population, 3,116 were enslaved, and the free Black population was 672. Other races or ethnic groups were not listed.[5]

What we do have is a special 1865 census after the Civil War done in Fairfax County by the Freedman's Bureau that goes into greater detail.

SUMMARY OF CENSUS RETURNS OF COLORED PEOPLE, FAIRFAX COUNTY, VIRGINIA, NOVEMBER 15TH, 1865

Blacks: 2,332
Mulattoes: 540
Quadroons: 60
Octoroons: 9
Total: 2,941

Males: 1,552
Females: 1,389

14 years of age and under: 1,121
Under 20 and over 14: 423
Under 50 and over 20: 1,140
Under 70 and over 50: 203
Over 70: 54

Status on Jany. 1st, 1863

Slave: 2,167
Free: 774
Resident: 2,878
Nonresident: 63
Laborers: 2,133
Mechanics: 27
Employed by government: 99
Employed by former owner: 163
Not employed: 274
Helped by government: 91
Able to read: 128
Unable to read: 2,813
Unable to support themselves: 539

Dramatic population changes came to Fairfax County in the middle of the twentieth century. In the 140 years from 1790 to 1930, the county's agrarian population doubled. In a mere twenty years, from 1930 to 1950, the number of inhabitants almost quadrupled, with 1930's population at 25,264, 1940's at 40,929 and 1950's at 98,557. Despite an increase in the Black population during this same period, their population percentage was not proportionally as high as that of the White population. For example, the 1940 census shows that the Black population was 6,695 (16%) and the White population was 34,234 (84%). In 1950, the Black population was 9,700 (9.8%) and the White population was 88,857 (89.6%). By 1960, the county's overall population had nearly tripled from the decade before, to 275,002. The increase in the Black population was noteworthy at 11,941, but the percentage of Black people within the county went down, at 4.8%.[6] In 1970, the total population of Fairfax County was 455,021, which included:

White: 424,114 (93.2%)
Black: 15,859 (3.5%)
Spanish: 11,623 (2.6%)
Asian: 1,833 (.4%)
American Indian: 427 (0.1%)
Other: 1,165 (0.2%)[7]

Why? The GI Bill, established in 1944, played an integral role in shaping post–World War II America. It enabled hundreds of thousands of men and women to get a higher education, many of whom could never have afforded it otherwise. The bill also helped build America's middle class, although it left many minority veterans behind. Fairfax County was no different. Post–World War II suburbs with model home communities were built one after the other for qualified veterans. White families flooded into the area due to the expansion of federal government jobs, causing an influx of veterans with work or school in Washington, D.C. It became a bedroom community rather than predominantly farmland.

Two important benefits of the GI Bill were that military veterans can qualify to cover costs for school and training; and two, VA Loans for first time home buyers.[8] This was not the case with African American veterans. President Truman signed Executive Order 9981 to desegregate the military on July 26, 1948. However, Black veterans were still limited in scholarship benefits to overcrowded Black-founded colleges or a handful of White colleges if they applied. There was not enough room for all those who wanted to attend. VA home equity loans backed by the federal government were denied to African Americans. This stifled their movement into Fairfax County.[9]

Fairfax County's African American communities were redlined into certain neighborhoods due to race. Therefore, Black veterans who came to work and live here were often connected by family, marriage, friends or work associates. The "hearth and home" enclosed segregated neighborhoods were paramount, where residents were surrounded by their families, neighbors, places of worship and educational institutions. The number of African Americans rose but not in proportion to the rest of the county.

The population of all races in the county increased year by year until COVID. Then, for the first time since Fairfax's founding, there was a decrease: from 1,150,309 in 2020 to 1,145,670 in 2021 and then to 1,138,331 in 2022. In 2021, the percentages of ethnic groups in Fairfax were as follows:

White: 49.1%
Asian: 20.5%
Hispanic/Latino: 16.6%
Black: 10.1%
Multiracial: 3.6%[10]

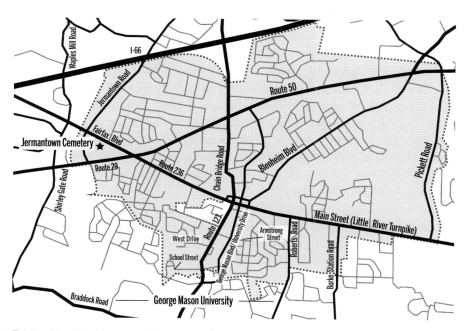

Fairfax City, Virginia map. *Map typeset by Sam Lindner and Arcadia Publishing.*

Fairfax city aerial map, 1927. Highlights: Center of town is where two roads intersect. One is Little River Turnpike (Main Street), going from bottom to top. The other road is Chain Bridge Road, going left to right. Adams Hotel, at the crossroads, looks a little like a two-tiered rectangular wedding cake, but it really is a four-story hotel with a veranda across it. The courthouse is across the street, shaded by trees. Looking to the left of the center on Chain Bridge Road, you will see a church with a steeple. That is the first African American Mount Calvary Church, built in 1870. *Courtesy of the Virginia Room, FCPL.*

The 1920 Adams Hotel is across the street from the Fairfax Courthouse in Fairfax, Virginia. If you had court business, especially lawyers and the like, this was where you stayed during court days. *Courtesy of the Virginia Room, FCPL.*

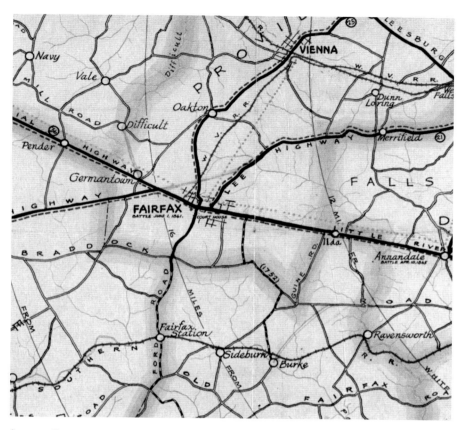

Surrounding area map of Fairfax, Virginia, 1927. The neighboring aerial map is positioned the same way and shows Fairfax City in the center. This map expands beyond the aerial map to show surrounding areas, including Germantown (Jermantown), to the left of the city center, and Ilda, to the right of the city center. *Federal Department of Transportation. Courtesy of the Virginia Room, FCPL.*

PART I.

JERMANTOWN CEMETERY

INTRODUCTION

by Constance B. Smith

On August 24, 1868, Jermantown Cemetery was purchased from William T. Rumsey, a prominent landowner, and his wife, Carolyn Rumsey, for use by the Colored Lodge No. 4 Burial Sons and Daughters of the Benevolence of Fairfax Court House, Virginia, to bury their dead. During this era, African Americans were not allowed to bury their dead in the larger cemetery known as the Fairfax City Cemetery. Rumsey then deeded the cemetery to Alfred Whaley, Thomas Sinkfield and Milton Brooks, freed African Americans, who became trustees on behalf of the colored Lodge No. 4 Burial Sons and Daughters of the Benevolence of Fairfax Court House, Virginia.

Much history is contained in this tiny one-acre cemetery, where century-old trees shade the graves of enslaved African Americans and their descendants. For over one hundred years, communities of people whose hard work helped to successfully develop Fairfax County, Virginia, were buried in the cemetery. They were laborers, farmers and field hands; cooks, laundresses and housekeepers; blacksmiths, carpenters and coopers; preachers, doctors and teachers; and soldiers.

There are nearly two hundred marked and unmarked graves. Final burials occurred in the 1990s.

The surnames of those known to be buried in Jermantown Cemetery are: Allison, Anderson, Arison, Bowls, Briggs, Brooks, Brown, Carrier, Carter, Chambers, Colbert, Collins, Conic, Early, Ferguson, Ford, Gibson, Groomes, Gunnell, Harris, Harrod, Hedgemon, Jackson, Johnson, Lamb,

Jermantown Cemetery sign on Wreath-Laying and Remembrance Event program. Sponsors: Descendants, Jermantown Cemetery Preservation Society, RRG (Christian racial unity group). *Courtesy of Jeanne Aviyorh.*

Lucas, Marshall, Martin, Morarity, Munsey, Murray, Neal, Nickens, Oliver, Parker, Payne, Payton, Runner, Simpson, Sinkfield, Tibbs, Whaley, Whislin, White and Winston.

Chapter 1

JERMANTOWN CEMETERY HISTORY

By Etta Willson, Rita Colbert, Linneall Naylor, Rondia Prescott and Jenee Lindner

In 1865, after the Civil War, African Americans in Fairfax wanted schools for their children, churches to worship in and a deeded cemetery for burying their dead. The city had a new cemetery after the Civil War, but African Americans were not allowed to be buried there.[11] Prejudice did not end overnight.

These stalwart, long-marginalized American citizens were supported in two ways: by the federal government and by their own Christian charitable organization. There were many likeminded segregated community organizations like this by other names, especially in the South. In the Washington, D.C. metro area, the organization African Americans joined was called the Benevolent Association or the African American Colored Brothers, Sisters, Sons, and Daughters of Benevolence Order Lodges. This national organization existed from 1838 to 1923, with several local chapters, including Fairfax Court House, Virginia.[12] It was a humanitarian organization started nationally before the Civil War by freed African Americans to help one another in times of need, through unemployment, health crises, natural disasters or other important community crises. The organization was nondenominational. It would be the Fairfax Court House Lodge No. 4 that would buy the Jermantown Cemetery plot of land. On May 30, 1873, the *Fairfax News* reported, on the "Brothers of Benevolence Order Colored Convention":

> *Rev. Jacob Ross, the colored preacher from Georgetown, D. C, called at our office one day last week, and submitted "proceedings of the Convention*

Mount Calvary Baptist Church, where David and Rondia Prescott were married in 1993. *Photo courtesy of Rondia Prescott.*

of the Order of Brothers, Sisters and Daughters of Benevolence," held at Fairfax C[ourt] H[ouse]., Va., May 2d, 1874.[13]

The Grand Lodge of the Order is located at Georgetown, D.C., with subordinate lodges at the following places: Fairfax Court House, Vienna, Lewinsville, Halls Hill, Leesburg, Houghsville, Middletown and the Point of Rocks. Here is a mass-produced handout that discussed more in depth the local umbrella Benevolent Association in the Washington, D.C. area, which included the No. 4 Lodge in Fairfax Court House, Virginia:[14]

WASHINGTON D.C. AREA BENEVOLENT ASSOCIATION, 1838–1923

"Experience has proved that the association of individuals and the formation of societies for the express purpose of benevolence, have

*seldom if ever failed to meet the sanction of both God and man…"
from the Constitution of the Free Young Men's Benevolent Association,
Washington, DC, founded in 1838.*[15]

*The Colored Union Benevolent Association established Mt. Pleasant
Plains Cemetery in 1870 at today's Walter Pierce Park. The group was
founded in October 1838 as the Free Young Men's Benevolent Association.
Like other Black fraternal organizations that arose in East Coast cities in
the early 19th century, its members aided one another in times of sickness,
unemployment and death.*

Before slavery was outlawed in the District [Washington, D.C.] *in
1862, the first criterion for Association membership was that a man be
free. Most members were previously enslaved. Others were born free, hailing
from some of Washington's earliest free African American families. The
Association was multi-denominational. Members were required to lead
exemplary lives: profanity, drunkenness and other undignified behavior
were grounds for expulsion. Despite city laws that banned secret meetings
among free Blacks, Association members agreed not to divulge details of
their meetings to outsiders.*

*Many Association men were related by birth or marriage. Many lived
in today's West End, Shaw, and Downtown neighborhoods, working as
government messengers, coach drivers, servants, and laborers. They were
activists. Members founded many of the city's first African American
schools, churches, and civic organizations. Some members—notably Charles
H. Brown (1805–1868)—waged early legal battles for civil rights,
challenging an oppressive set of city laws known as the "Black Code." In
1848, Association members were deeply involved in Washington's largest
known Underground Railroad escape attempt, when 77 enslaved men,
women and children secretly boarded the schooner* Pearl *near the Seventh
Street wharf in hope of sailing north to freedom.*

*The Association established its first burial ground in 1849 at 12th and
V streets, NW, operating the "Free Young Men's Burying Ground" until
1870. Then the Association purchased 6.75 acres of land next to Rock
Creek from the son of John Quincy Adams, who had owned a mill at the
site. The new "Mt. Pleasant Plains Cemetery" abutted the city's only
Quaker cemetery, founded in 1807. Mt. Pleasant Plains quickly became
one of Washington's busiest African American cemeteries, providing burial
spots for as many as 10,000 people until its forced closure in 1890. The
Colored Union Benevolent Association was dissolved in 1923.*[16]

FREEDMAN BUREAU OR BUREAU OF REFUGEES, FREEDMEN AND ABANDONED LANDS

During the colonial period, public officials, such as court clerks, made their living by collecting fees for services rendered. During the 18th century, clerks began receiving a salary in addition to these fees. Services provided by the Clerk of Court included recording documents, issuing court orders, taking depositions, making inventories, processing estates, and keeping records of births, deaths and marriages. Today's circuit court clerks' duties are similar, such as recording deeds, wills and marriage licenses, keeping court records and ensuring court case procedures follow legal guidelines.[17]

The national government supported them during the occupation after the Civil War with enforcement through their federal agency called the Bureau of Refugees, Freedmen, and Abandoned Lands or Freedmen's Bureau from 1865–1872.[18]

It was tasked with providing immediate assistance to blacks in the form of food, clothing and arranging contracts for renting houses and land for farming. The Freedmen's Bureau also was relied on by blacks for protection from acts of violence and for the first time the public education of their children. Following male blacks being granted suffrage by Congress in March 1867, the Bureau also sought to ensure black participation in local, state, and national politics.[19]

The Freedmen's Bureau was headquartered in the old Fairfax courthouse on the corner of Main Street (Little River Turnpike) and Chain Bridge Road. The bureau protected new citizens in cases of unlawful coercion. Therefore, in Fairfax Court House, the first Black churches were built only a block away.

In August 1865, George Amos, the first agent of the bureau, was tasked to take the first census of the county's Black population. Of the 2,941 Blacks reported to be living in Fairfax County in 1865, none were living in the Freedmen's Village in Arlington, where many escaped ex-enslaved people from the South had fled. There were at least three communities in which freed African Americans had gathered. There was a group of about 30 at Lewinsville, about 30 at Fairfax Station and about 130 at Fairfax Court House Area, including the Village of Ilda (and Jermantown). The others were scattered around, with many of them still living where they had

Fairfax Courthouse was completed in 1800. It was located at the crossroads of the county. Going east–west was Little River Turnpike, going north–south was the ancient Ox Road/ Chain Bridge Road used by animals and Indigenous people. The location was also chosen for its rise on the top of a small ridge, to avoid issues with flooding. It had excellent spring water for people and animals. It became an all-important gathering place for court days and other community events. *Photo by Jenee Lindner.*

always lived, on the lands of former slave owners.[20] (Additional breakdown in the book introduction.)

The bureau helped when any complaints were reported. Even after the war ended in April 1865, some were still in bondage against their will for months or years afterward. Here are some examples:

Bureau R.R. & A.L.
Headquarters 5th District of VA
Alexandria, Virginia, Sept. 4, 1865
Special Order No. 9

Capt. Geo. A. Armes, will immediately proceed to the house of Mrs. Nancy Ratcliffe and bring away the two colored children Sarah and Fannie Harper, who are still held as slave by said Mrs. R., and deliver them to this office. If it is necessary to take them by force—or even bloodshed—let it be done. The purpose of the Bureau must and shall be carried out so far as it is in the power of the Supt. of this District.

Capt. Armes will attend to this matter in person and if he has not sufficient force at his command, he will call on Capt. Baker, at Vienna, for men.

James I. Ferree, Act. Supt. 5th District VA[21]

Headquarters Military Governor Alexandria, Va., October 10, 1865
Lieut. Smith Asst. Supt. & C.
Lieut.

The bearer of this is, Amelia Bolding from Washington, D.C., she has a little niece, at one Mr. R. Ford's of Fairfax Court House, who refuses to give up the little girl. If it is so that you can, please send one soldier & have him take the child from Mr. Ford & deliver her to this woman. If you can it would be well to send her to the C.H. in your wagon. Then send her to the station.

I am, Lieut.
Very Respectfully &c.
J.W. Bushong
Actg. Supt, 5th Dist., Va.[22]

November 29, 1865
Bureau of Refugees Freedmen and Abandoned Lands
Vienna VA
Mr. Richard Johnson

Dear Sir:

Mr. Alfred Whaley Colored states that you have in your possession the key of the cellar or room where he has potatoes and storage which is necessary for his immediate use, and that you refuse to give to him the key that he may get in the room where they are kept next.

I trust Mr. Johnson that if this be a correct statement in regard to this affair that you will not persist in this manner of action towards Mr. Whaley.

It is very unpleasant for me to be compelled by duty to interfere in matters of this kind but this man's rights must be respected. You will please give him the key, or he will be obliged to use other means regarding the above-mentioned room.

I am Sir Very Respectfully, Your Obedient Servant,
Sidney B Smith
1st Lieut. V.R.C. Asst. Supt.,
1st Division, 5th District of Virginia[23]

Not dependent on charity, the freedmen had few problems finding suitable work. By November 1865, not one Fairfax County African American was dependent on the charity of the bureau. Wages were about five dollars a month for women and about ten dollars a month for men, the same rate they had been before the Civil War.[24]

Orin Hine was the Freedmen's Bureau superintendent in Fairfax Courthouse, Virginia, by 1867.[25] In the fall of 1867, he and Judge Job Hawxhurst were delegates to the Virginia Constitutional Convention headed by Judge John C. Underwood. The purpose of the convention was to write a new constitution for the State of Virginia. Both Hine and Hawxhurst played leading roles at the convention. Hine, Hawxhurst and Underwood were all originally from New York state, having come to northern Virginia prior to the Civil War. Their common heritage and war experiences significantly influenced the decisions that the convention took with respect to the future of Virginia's government in the postwar era.[26] Fairfax County justice of the peace Job Hawxhurst especially, would facilitate with his signature the Jermantown Cemetery purchase.

1868: PURCHASING THE JERMANTOWN CEMETERY, FAIRFAX, VIRGINIA

William and Caroline Rumsey sold and transferred one acre of their land for forty dollars to the Fairfax Court House Virginia Lodge No. 4 on August 24, 1868. The designated trustees took possession and administrated the cemetery on behalf of Lodge No. 4 Colored Burial Sons and Daughters of Benevolence of Fairfax Courthouse, namely Alfred Whaley, Thomas Sinkfield and Milton Brooks.[27] It is believed to have been a graveyard already.[28] The land deed gave this cemetery new owners, who formally named it Jermantown Cemetery after the interracial community named Jermantown where it was located.[29]

> *Dated: August 24, 1868.*
>
> *Transfer of the burial area (Jermantown Cemetery) from William T. Rumsey and his wife, Caroline, to the Burial Sons and Daughters of Benevolence of Fairfax Court House Virginia—recorded in Fairfax Deed Book 1–4, page 429.*
>
> *"This Deed made this twenty-fourth day of August, Eighteen-hundred and sixty-eight, between William T. Rumsey and Caroline his wife of the County of Fairfax, state of Virginia of the one part and Alfred Whaley, Thomas Sinkfield and Milton Brooks Trustees for and in behalf of the Burial Sons and Daughters of Benevolence of Fairfax Court House Virginia of the other part. Witnesses, that for and in consideration of the sum of Forty dollars in hand paid the receipt where of is hereby acknowledged, the said William T. Rumsey and Caroline his wife hath bargained, sold and granted in fee, a certain piece or parcel of land lying on the Little River Turnpike about one mile west of Fairfax Court House, beginning at the corner between the lands of Samuel Brown and William T. Rumsey on the South side of said Turnpike and extending with the said Turnpike West seventy yards, and extending back South binding on the land of said Brown a sufficient distance to make one acre; unto the said Alfred Whaley, Thomas Sinkfield and Milton Brooks Trustees as aforesaid and their lawful successors for the use of the said Burial Sons and Daughters of Benevolence and to their sole use and benefit forever.*
>
> *To have and to hold the same free from all claim or claims of the said William T. Rumsey and Caroline his wife their heirs or assigns forever. And the said William T. Rumsey and Caroline his wife for themselves, their heirs or assigns further doth covenant and agree with the said Alfred Whaley,*

430

West of Fairfax Court House, beginning at the corner
between the Lands of Samuel Brown and William D Rumsey
on the South side of said Turnpike and extending with
the said Turnpike West twenty yards, and extending
back South binding on the land of said Brown a suf=
ficient distance to make one acre; unto the said Alfred
Whaley, Thomas Sinkfield and Milton Brooks Trustees as
aforesaid and their lawful successors for the use of the said
Colored Burial Sons and Daughters of Benevolence and
to their sole use and benefit forever

To have and to hold the same free from all claim or
claims of the said William D Rumsey and Caroline his
wife their heirs or assigns forever. And the said William
D Rumsey and Caroline his wife for themselves, their heirs
or assigns further doth covenant and agree with the said
Alfred Whaley, Thomas Sinkfield and Milton Brooks
Trustees as aforesaid and their lawful successors as
Trustees aforesaid that they have the right to convey
the said land and that they do by these presents against
the lawful claim or claims of themselves, their heirs or assigns
or of any person whatsoever forever warrant and defend. It is
further understood and agreed that should the grantees
fail to keep the said piece of land fenced, the said grantor
shall never be liable for any damage arising from any
trespass of any stock belonging to him on the land hereby
conveyed. In witness whereof we have hereunto set our
hands and seals the day and year first above written.

Wm D Rumsey Seal
Caroline Rumsey Seal

Fairfax County To wit.

I Job Hawxhurst a Justice of the
Peace in and for the County aforesaid do hereby certify that
William D Rumsey whose name is signed to the foregoing
deed bearing date the 24th day of August 1868, personally
appeared before me and acknowledged the same to his

Deed of sale for Jermantown Cemetery in 1868. *Fairfax Deed Book 1–4, p. 430. Courtesy of Fairfax Circuit Court Historic Records Center.*

Thomas Sinkfield and Milton Brooks Trustees as aforesaid that they have the right to convey the said land and that they do by these presents against the lawful claim or claims of themselves, their heirs or assigns or of any person whatsoever forever warrant and defend. This further understood and agreed that should the grantees fail to keep the said piece of land fenced the said grantor shall never be liable for any damages arising from any trespass of any stock belonging to him in the land hereby conveyed. In witness whereof we have hereunto set our hands and seals this day and year first above written."

Wm. T. Rumsey, Caroline Rumsey
J.D. Richardson, Clerk of the Court
"Due hereby certify…"
Job Hawxhurst, Fairfax County Justice of the Peace[30]

Thus was established a community burial ground for the African American residents of Fairfax Court House. Today, there are about fifty stone markers in existence for more than one hundred graves known of today. Many were buried under wooden crosses that have long since worn away, or they were buried under rocks placed above them.

We believe this was a graveyard before the Civil War, created for the servants of and people enslaved by Richard Ratcliffe, owner of Mount Vineyard Plantation, where the cemetery is located.[31] Before the Civil War, the enslaved were not allowed to write their names on a grave marker of any kind, even if they could read and write. To read and write was illegal in many southern states, including Virginia. The enslaved would be punished if they wrote on the marker, in any way, the deceased's name. But now the Civil War was over. This changed the trajectory in a dramatic way toward giving voice to those who once had no voice in the public square.

EARLY JERMANTOWN CEMETERY TRUSTEES

The three cemetery trustees originally appointed in 1868 on behalf of Lodge No. 4, Sons and Daughters of Benevolence were Alfred Whaley (1830–1891), Thomas Sinkfield (1823–1896) and Milton Brooks (1809–1896). In the next twenty-five years, they would be replaced by Jack Rowe (1824–after 1909), Horace Gibson (1817–1921), Strother Gibson (1846–1927) and James Henderson.[32] Eventually, all of these serving trustees died without successors.

Christmas memorial wreath-laying ceremony at Jermantown Cemetery, December 2022. Catherine Goode (*right*) is a direct descendant of founding cemetery trustee Alfred Whaley. On the left is Linneall Naylor, direct descendant of founding cemetery trustees Thomas Sinkfield and Milton Brooks. *Photo courtesy of Tony Zipfel.*

ALFRED WHALEY (1830–1891), TRUSTEE

Alfred Whaley was born in 1830 in Providence, Fairfax, Virginia, and died on November 22, 1891[33] in Fairfax County, Virginia. He was buried in the Jermantown Cemetery.[34] The *Fairfax Herald* reported:

> *Alfred Whaley, an intelligent colored citizen, and who is a good blacksmith, residing at Germantown, two miles west of the C[ourt] H[ouse], has beets growing in his garden there that measure 2 feet 7 inches in circumference. That beet can't be beat.*[35]

Whaley's family continued to live on the old Mellontree plantation area in Jermantown. Formally enslaved, now free, in the 1870 census, he and his family are listed (misspelled) as Alfred Wholey, age forty-eight; his wife, Matilda Wholey, age fifty-two; their son Charles Wholey, age twenty-one; their son John Wholey, age eighteen; their daughter Lizzie Wholey, age twelve; their daughter Mollie Wholey, age ten; their son Thomas Wholey, age eight; and their daughter Alice Wholey, age five.[36]

In 1869, Whaley would buy two acres of land two doors down from the cemetery, across from present Bevin Drive and Jermantown Road. He purchased the land from William Rumsey, the same person who sold the Jermantown Cemetery land to the trustees the year before.[37]

In the 1880 census, Whaley and his wife are listed with only their son, Thomas Whaley, age nineteen.[38] Whaley is listed as age fifty-four and a blacksmith.[39] Whaley's family also sold farm goods to locals and travelers along the Little River Turnpike.[40] The toll gate was where all people must stop and pay to use the Little River Turnpike in the Jermantown area. It was close to the Whaleys, with ready customers.[41] Whaley must have done quite well for himself. In 1883, he bought an additional 1 acre and 120 square poles of land across the street from Jesse Clark, an African American neighbor.[42]

THOMAS SINKFIELD (1823–1896), TRUSTEE

The next Jermantown Cemetery trustee was Thomas Sinkfield (1823–1896), born free and son of a free African American man from Loudoun County, Virginia.[43] In the 1870 and 1880 censuses, he was listed as a close neighbor of Alfred Whaley's family in Fairfax, Virginia (called Providence at the time).[44] According to the 1880 census (in which his last name was misspelled as "Sinkuen"), he was fifty-seven years old. His wife's maiden name was Mary Ellen Murphy, age forty-nine. Sinkfield's occupation was laborer, and he could not write. His household included children Richard, age twenty-one; Mary, age seventeen; Josephine, age fifteen; Virginia, age thirteen; Frances, age nine; and Howard, age seven.[45] The family made their living by selling food to drovers and herders along the Little River Turnpike.[46]

At some point, Sinkfield and several of his children moved to Steelton, near Philadelphia, Pennsylvania, to live with his daughter Jennie (Virginia) V. Sinkfield (1867–1952) and her husband, Arthur Albert Harrod (1868–1934). Harrod was also from Providence, Fairfax, Virginia. Thomas Sinkfield came back to Fairfax sometime before his death.[47] He would be buried in Jermantown, having died on September 30, 1896.[48]

Thomas Sinkfield's daughter Frances Alvernal Sinkfield, who went by the nickname Fannie, was born around 1872 in Virginia to Thomas Sinkfield and his wife, Mary. In 1888 and 1889, she appears in the Howard University catalog as a "Normal School" student, meaning she was studying to become a teacher.[49] She did not move to Pennsylvania with her other siblings.

Frances Sinkfield first appears in Fairfax County Public School records in the fall of 1889, when she was assigned to teach at the Chantilly "Colored" School (then known as Number B) in Dranesville District. Frances taught school at Chantilly for two years; then, in 1891, she began teaching in the town of Vienna, which had recently incorporated and formed its own school district apart from Providence District. Articles in the *Fairfax Herald* confirm that Frances Sinkfield taught at Vienna during the 1891–92 and 1893–94 school years.[50]

In September 1900, Frances married Robert "Edward" Brent in Passaic, New Jersey. The couple had two children, Howard and Vivian. They eventually settled in Washington, D.C. After the death of her second husband, Frances married a third time, in 1919, to John W. Ransell. Frances Sinkfield passed away in February 1953 in Washington, D.C., and was buried in Vienna, Virginia.[51]

MILTON GEORGE BROOKS (1809–1896), TRUSTEE

Milton Brooks was a farmer and the third Jermantown Cemetery trustee. He was enslaved until the Civil War and reportedly buried at Jermantown Cemetery. Agnes Brooks, Milton's wife, also formerly enslaved, has a headstone that says "1812–1872." DNA from Agnes Brooks's descendants shows a familial relationship with two plantation owners' families, Ratcliffe and Fitzhugh. Therefore, Brooks's true last name may have been Ratcliffe or Fitzhugh. We also have 1891 death listings for a Charles Brooks, perhaps his brother, an eighty-year-old "Colored" (Black) laborer, who was born in 1811 and died of old age on December 20, 1891, in Centerville, Fairfax, Virginia.[52]

Milton and Agnes had two daughters. Their first daughter was Margaret (1827–1911), who married Horace Gibson (1817–1921). This couple played a prominent role in the Black community, with twelve children born to their union. Many of their progeny are buried in Jermantown Cemetery.[53] Horace Gibson and their oldest son, Strother Gibson, would later become cemetery trustees. Their daughter Eveline (1849–1927) married Joshua Ray Murray on April 28, 1870. They would have ten children. Many of their progeny are buried there. Eveline's death certificate calls her father George (not Milton) Brooks and her mother Agnes Brooks. It lists both parents as born in Richmond, Virginia.[54]

JACK ROWE (1824–AFTER 1909), TRUSTEE

Before 1887, it was clear there had been a trusteeship change. We don't know when Milton Brooks resigned and was replaced by Jack Rowe. It might have been due to Milton Brooks's old age. The three trustees now were Jack Rowe, Alfred Whaley, and Thomas Sinkfield.[55]

The following is the text of a June 25, 1909 article in the *Alexandria Gazette* that included the photograph of Jack Rowe at right:

> *Everybody hereabouts who is anybody knows old "Uncle" Jack Rowe, whose picture adorns this article. Indeed, Uncle Jack is not only known, by everybody, but is known to fame as well; for he enjoys the unique distinction of having found the body of Capt. John Q. Marr, the first man killed in the Civil War in actual battle. When Lieutenant (now Brigadier General, retired) Tompkins, in command of some United States dragoons, made his celebrated dash into this town a little before dawn of day, June 1st, 1861, a lively fight ensued, and when the morning sunbeams dispelled the darkness, revealing an excited populace and more or less demoralized troops, it was found that John Q. Marr, captain of the Warrenton Rifles, was missing.*
>
> *It was not long before "Uncle" Jack discovered his dead body lying in some tall grass just back of where the M.E. Church, South, now stands. That gallant gentleman had been killed while bringing his company to the scene of conflict. "Uncle" Jack, it will be observed, is posed in a restful and graceful attitude. It must not be inferred, however, that he is constitutionally tired, for he has not a lazy bone in his body; He is a worthy old man, of the old school of colored people now so rapidly disappearing from view, and, before the war, belonged to Mr. Thomas Moore, father of Hon. R. Walton Moore. He is in the 85th year of his age and enjoys the respect and esteem of all who know him.*

Rowe lived with his mother and worked as a handyman, an assistant to Clerk of the Court Thomas Moore and a farmhand. After the Civil War, he lived for a time in Alexandria and then returned to Fairfax Court House. He never married.[56]

Right: This photograph of Jack Rowe was taken by J. Harry Shannon in 1909, when Rowe was eighty-five. He is sitting against the old Fairfax Courthouse well pillar. *From* This Was Virginia 1900–1927 as Shown by Glass Negatives of J. Harry Shannon, the Rambler, *compiled by Connie and Mayo Stuntz. Courtesy of the Virginia Room, FCPL.*

Below: Old Fairfax Courthouse well. It was known in the area for the sweet spring water for man and beast. It was an informal meeting place. "Let's meet at the courthouse well!" was a common phrase. *Courtesy of Jenee Lindner, who owns the 1909 postcard.*

Jermantown Cemetery Trusteeship Document, 1887

An 1887 Jermantown Cemetery trusteeship document was presented to the Fairfax County Circuit Court docket requesting new trustees. Jack Rowe, Whaley and Sinkfield were asked to retire. The reason for the request was negligence on the part of the Jermantown Cemetery trustees. The petitioners wished to appoint new trustees: Horace Gibson, Strother Gibson and James Henderson.[57]

Alfred Whaley was quite elderly at that time and would die a few years later, in 1891. Sinkfield may have already left the area and moved in with his daughter and son-in-law residing in Pennsylvania. The complaint was signed by seventeen Lodge No. 4 Burial Sons and Daughters of Benevolence of Fairfax Court House Virginia descendants in support of a change, including Daniel Chambers, Maggie Chambers, Lewis Jackson, Joshua R. Murray, Evaline Murray, Margaret Dixon, Sarah J. Hunter, Charles Bronaugh, Nancy Bronaugh, Martin Mellontree, John A. Mellontree, Lewis Simms, Page Parker, Martha Simms, Jamie Garrett, Thomas Whiten and Joshua Pearson.[58]

Fairfax Circuit Court judge John Keith ruled in favor of the complainants.

Horace Gibson (1817–1912), Trustee

The next Jermantown Cemetery trustee, Horace Gibson (1817–1912), was born in Culpeper, Virginia, and with his partner, Moses Parker, he founded the Ilda community, east of downtown Fairfax on the Little River Turnpike. He married Milton Brooks's daughter Margaret Brooks (1827–1911) in 1846. Ilda has a well-documented history, thanks to the research of the founders' descendants Hareem Badil-Abish and Dennis Howard. Ilda began when Horace Gibson, the son of a Culpeper slave owner, bought his freedom and moved up north in the 1860s. He and his wife, Margaret, stayed in a shantytown on the Fitzhughs' land off Guinea Road. In 1868, he purchased five acres of land from Peter and Margarette Gooding near Guinea Road and the Little River Turnpike. The community was later named Ilda after Matilda Gibson Parker, who was Gibson's daughter.

Horace Gibson and his future business partner Moses Parker were trained blacksmiths and wheelwrights—specialized craftsmen who worked on wooden wheels and carriages. Their lucrative trade was rarely available to Black workers because White artisans would block them from training in

Old man traveling locally on Little River Turnpike Road in 1921. *From* This Was Virginia 1900–1927 as Shown by Glass Negatives of J. Harry Shannon, the Rambler, *compiled by Connie and Mayo Stuntz. Courtesy of the Virginia Room, FCPL.*

Fairfax County map that includes Jermantown, Fairfax and Ilda, where three segregated communities thrived and endured. *Courtesy of the Library of Congress.*

the field. After moving to the area, Gibson and Parker established a highly successful blacksmith shop conveniently located on the Little River Turnpike Toll Road. Customers from all races and classes visited the shop on their way to or from Fairfax, Alexandria or Washington, D.C.[59]

STROTHER GIBSON (1846–1927), TRUSTEE

Horace Gibson's oldest son, Strother Gibson (1846–1927), was born in Culpeper, Virginia. He married Martha Weir Davis in 1868. They had eleven children: Samuel Strother, Louisa, William, Lavinia, Thomas, Morris, Margaret, Horace, Adeline, Martha and Robert. Strother Gibson worked as a personal aide to the prosperous Willard family and managed their estate, Layton Hall. He was a founding trustee of the Mount Calvary Baptist Church and was elected as a delegate to the state congressional convention in 1892.[60] He died a year after his wife on October 18, 1926, and was buried with his wife in the Jermantown Cemetery.[61]

JAMES HENDERSON, TRUSTEE

The oldest son of Milton George Whaley, Charles Whaley (1849–?), married Pauline Henderson.[62] We believe it was her father, this James Henderson, who became a Jermantown Cemetery trustee in 1887.[63]

> *Pauline A. Henderson, age 22; Birth Date: 1851; Marriage Date: 15 May 1873; Marriage License Place: Fairfax; Person performing the Ceremony: Marshall* [probably Marshall D. Williams, first Pastor of Mount Calvary Baptist Church]*; Parent 1: James Henderson; Parent 2: Emeline Henderson; Spouse: Charles W. Whaley.*[64]

FAIRFAX COLORED CEMETERY ASSOCIATION
BY ETTA WILLSON

By 1927, all the trustees had died, and the Benevolence Association had gone out of existence in 1923.[65] Etta Willson alerted us to the fact, per a *Washington Post* article she has in her family collections, that there was a new cemetery organization created. On January 24, 1930, Walter Bowles, George Hunter, James Hunter, Ellen Gray and Antonia Payne were approved by the Fairfax County Circuit Court. They were verified to replace the Benevolence Society.[66]

Antonia Payne (July 14, 1867–May 23, 1939)

Antonia Payne was born in Fairfax, Virginia. She was the wife of Robert Payne. They had two children: Virgil and Myrtle. Payne was the daughter of James and Sarah Jane Hunter. She was a well-respected citizen in the

Inthe Circuit Court for Fairfax County, Virginia.

In re appointment of Trustees for Fairfax Colored:

Cemetery Association............................: At Law- January Term, 1930.

This matter coming on this day to be heard upon the petition filed by the parties interested in the operation, maintenance and upkeep of the Fairfax Colored Cemetery requesting the appointment of Walter Bowles, George Hunter, James Hunter, Ellen Gray and Antonia Payne, as Trustees for the Fairfax Colored Cemetery Association, for and in the place and stead of the former Trustees, all of whom are dead,upon consideration whereof, the Court doth now grant the prayer of the said petition, and doth now appoint as trustees of the said Cemetery Association, Walter Bowles, George Hunter,

January 20th, 1930

James Hunter, Ellen Gray and Antonia Payne, for and in the place and stead of the deceased Trustees, and doth now vest them with all the powers and impose upon them all of the duties of the original Trustees as provided in Chapter 7 of the Code of this State.

//

To Meet Next Week

The Fairfax County Colored Citizens Association will hold its regular meeting in the colored church, at Merrifield, Wednesday, January 19, at 8 p. m. Matters in reference to the colored high school are to be considered and a good speaker is expected to be present and to give a talk.

Above: Fairfax Colored Cemetery Association. *Fairfax Minute Book 14, p. 116. Courtesy of Fairfax Circuit Court Historic Records Center.*

Left: *Fairfax Herald*, January 14, 1938. Fairfax County Colored Citizens Association. *Courtesy of the Virginia Room, FCPL.*

community who was very active in civic, church and social affairs. She also served as assistant secretary of the Fairfax School League, which was part of the Rosenwald School in Fairfax. Payne was a member of Mount Calvary Baptist Church, where she served faithfully. She is buried at Jermantown Cemetery alongside her husband, Robert.

Ellen Gray (December 29, 1880–February 15, 1946)

Ellen Gray was born in Fairfax, Virginia. She was the wife of Ernest Gray and the daughter of William and Lucinda Lucas. Gray was very active in school and church work. She was a member of Mount Calvary Baptist Church, where she served as superintendent of the Sunday school. Gray was also known in the community as an accomplished seamstress. She is buried at Jermantown Cemetery where her husband, Ernest, is also interred.

James Hunter (December 24, 1880–March 2, 1957)

James Hunter was born in Fairfax, Virginia. He was married to Gertrude Horton Hunter. They had four children: Edith, Herman, Alvin and Warren. He was the son of James and Sarah Nealle Hunter.

George Hunter (February 1, 1891–June 1, 1947)

George Hunter was born in Fairfax, Virginia. He was the son of Robert and Margaret Moriarty Hunter. He is buried in Jermantown.

Walter Bowles (December 6, 1886–May 4, 1967)

Walter Bowles was born in Fairfax, Virginia. He was married to Susie Clark Bowles. They had eleven children: Kathleen, Purvis, Haywood, Bernice, Etta, Janie, Agnes, Walter Jr., Lillian, Alice and Geneva. Agnes and Walter Jr. are buried at Jermantown Cemetery. Walter Bowles was the son of Daniel and Roberta Hampton Bowles. The U.S. Census records for 1920–30 indicate he was employed as a porter with the old Washington and Virginia Railroad Company, founded in 1896. The railroad was originally horse drawn before electricity was used in the early 1900s. At the height of electric rail trolley operations, lines extended from Falls Church, Alexandria, Arlington and Fairfax. A ticket cost four cents. By 1937, the electric trolley era was over. The 1950 census indicates Bowles was self-employed as a lumberman. He was active in the community and a well-respected citizen who also participated in the local NAACP chapter.

We have several military veterans buried at Jermantown Cemetery. Three are highlighted here.

GEORGE LAMB, CIVIL WAR

1834–March 19, 1926

An 1855 entry from the Fairfax County Register of Free Blacks indicates that George Lamb was a free mulatto born to a free mother in Fairfax County sometime around 1834.[67] According to an obituary from the *Fairfax Herald*, Lamb, who was widely known as Uncle George, worked on various farms throughout the county. When the Civil War broke out, Captain William Dulany of Company D, Seventeenth Virginia Infantry (the Fairfax Rifles) brought Lamb with him as a body servant. (Dulany was the Unionist Fairfax delegate to the Virginia Convention.) It is not certain whether Lamb worked for Dulany prior to the war or whether he was hired specifically to come with Dulany.[68]

Lamb remained with the Seventeenth Virginia throughout the war, even after Dulany was severely wounded at Blackburn's Ford in 1861. Presumably,

Opposite: Old Fairfax looking down Main Street in about 1900. *Courtesy of the Virginia Room, FCPL.*

Above: Fairfax today, looking down Main Street. *Photo courtesy of Jenee Lindner.*

Lamb continued to serve with the regiment as a servant of some sort. The website for the Fairfax Rifles Living History Society also notes that there were five other Blacks "who served with the Confederacy from Fairfax County."[69]

After the Civil War, Lamb worked as a blacksmith for Joseph Cooper, who ran a wagon shop in Fairfax. Lamb never married and died in 1926. He is buried at Jermantown Cemetery.

> *George C. Lamb "Uncle George" Body Servant of Capt. William H. Dulaney, Co. D, 17th Va Inf. He was born in Fairfax in 1834, son of _____ and Harriet Lamb; a free negro who served throughout the Civil War with the 17th Va Infantry. After the war he was a blacksmith in the wagon shop of Joseph Cooper, Fairfax Courthouse. He died 3/19/1926 [of] "influenza" at the home of Winfield Runner on Fairfax—Centreville Rd. (Lee Hwy) and [was] buried at the Jermantown Cemetery. He had a Confederate military pension.*[70]

JAMES A. HARRIS, PRIVATE, U.S. MARINE CORPS, KOREAN WAR

October 13, 1930–December 21, 1973

Private James Alfred Harris, the son of Alphonso and Virginia Harris, was born on October 13, 1930, in Fairfax, Virginia. He attended public school in Fairfax County. James married Phyllis Marie Allen in 1951 and was a loving father to three daughters, Cynthia, Gwendolyn and Terry.

James A. Harris, PVT, USMC. Jermantown Cemetery. *Photo courtesy of Jenee Lindner.*

James enlisted in the United States Marine Corps during the Korean War on January 22, 1952. He was honorably discharged, due to an injury, on June 3, 1952.

James died on December 21, 1973, and is buried alongside his parents and two siblings, Maurice and Sylvia, in the Historic Jermantown Cemetery in Fairfax, Virginia.

MAURICE WATSON HARRIS, CORPORAL, U.S. ARMY, KOREAN WAR

February 10, 1928–June 2, 1991

Corporal Maurice Watson Harris, the son of Alphonso and Virginia Harris, was born on February 10, 1928, in Fairfax, Virginia.[71] He attended public school in Fairfax County. Maurice enlisted in the United States Army during the Korean War on October 24, 1950, and was honorably discharged on October 23, 1952. He died on June 2, 1991, and is buried, alongside his parents and two siblings, James and Sylvia, in the Historic Jermantown Cemetery, Fairfax, Virginia.

Maurice Watson Harris, corporal, U.S. Army, Korean War. Jermantown Cemetery. *Photo courtesy of Jenee Lindner.*

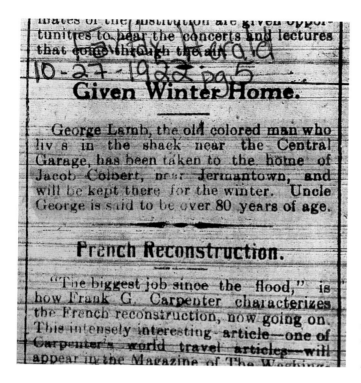

George Lamb, from the *Fairfax Herald*, October 27, 1922. *Courtesy of Etta Willson.*

Text from the newspaper clipping:

Fairfax Herald
10-27-1922 pg 5

Given Winter Home.

George Lamb, the old colored man who lives in the shack near the Central Garage, has been taken to the home of Jacob Colbert, near Jermantown, and will be kept there for the winter. Uncle George is said to be over 80 years of age.

French Reconstruction.

"The biggest job since the flood," is how Frank G. Carpenter characterizes the French reconstruction, now going on. This intensely interesting article—one of Carpenter's world travel articles—will appear in the Magazine of The Washing...

...mates of the institution are given opportunities to hear the concerts and lectures that come through the...

THE END OF AN ERA

By the 1970s, church members that had ancestors buried in Jermantown Cemetery took over the duties of cleanup and burials there. A Mount Calvary Baptist Church deacon and church trustee named Emmett Anderson remembers church groups going over to the cemetery in the 1980s to clean it.[72] Mount Calvary Baptist Church would hold funerals at the church and then move to this burial ground, a few miles away, for burial. There are no burials there now; the cemetery is full. In 1989, Reverend Booker tried to have the site listed on the Virginia Historic Register.

"Church Wants Cemetery Put on Historic Register"
By B.K. Morris
The Connection, 1989

Concern over the future of a Civil War-era, all-black cemetery in the City of Fairfax has prompted members of the Mount Calvary Baptist Church to appeal to the City Council to have the site declared a historical landmark.

Rev. Booker Taylor of Mount Calvary Baptist Church in Fairfax, VA. *Photo courtesy of Jeffery Johnson Jr.*

According to Rev. Booker Taylor, pastor of the church, located on School Street, parishioners are concerned that developers may be interested in building on the site. A historic designation would help assure the descendants of people buried there that the graves would not be moved in the future.

"The Jermantown Cemetery was established in 1868 in order to provide burial sites for former slaves who were denied burial in other cemeteries," said Taylor. "It's a symbol that black folk were here at a time when they were treated as non-persons."

The half-acre cemetery is located on Main Street (Route 236) west of the intersection with Lee Highway. It is bordered by a Giant supermarket and office condominiums.

According to Taylor, most of the more than forty gravestones in the cemetery are well maintained, but others are leaning over and faded. Several families, such as the Runners and Conics, have several generations buried there.

The cemetery originally belonged to the former slaves who established it, but their families died out without passing ownership to anyone, said Taylor. City workers mow the grass and church members perform additional maintenance, he said.

The cemetery has been full since 1970, said Taylor.

Mayor George T. Snyder Jr. said he asked the city's planning office to start working on getting the cemetery registered. Snyder said he knows of no developers interested in building on the cemetery site.

City planning director Peggy Wagner said the city would hire a consultant to prepare applications to the National Register of Historic Landmarks.

Mable Colbert is one of 137 area residents who signed a petition asking historical status for the cemetery. Colbert's parents and grandmother are buried there.

"As far as [parishioners] know, it would be the first all-black cemetery listed as a historic landmark in the state," said Colbert. "It's important evidence for future generations to look back on to know that their people have been in the city a long time," she said.

It did not happen. However, as of this writing, the new mayor of Fairfax City, Catherine Read, and the Fairfax City Historical Resources are doing the heavy lifting to get it done by 2025.

Chapter 2

A NEW BEGINNING

By Jenee Lindner

Starting in the 2000s, the City of Fairfax assumed primary care for Jermantown Cemetery site, assisted by local citizens.[73] In 2013, a *Washington Post* article called "Fairfax Moves Forward with Cemetery by the Poor" stated that the Jermantown Cemetery had been used for several years as a pauper's field after the last burial was done by the Black community.[74] This would have created havoc for genealogists trying to find graves specific to Black family descendants. Author Jenee Lindner checked with the Fairfax County Department of Family Services and determined this not to be true. The article correctly sited the county pauper's field on Jermantown Road. However, it is called the Fairfax County Pauper's Field, not Jermantown Cemetery, which is on Route 123. They are miles apart.[75]

Dennis Howard, using the sponsorship of his nonprofit called the Jermantown Cemetery Grave Preservation Society, formed a new trusteeship. This new Jermantown Cemetery trusteeship was approved by Fairfax County Circuit Court judge Jane Marum Roush on October 17, 2014.[76] The trustees included Dennis Howard (now deceased) as chair, Juan Bell, Sharon Gibson, Shakira Howard, Aiesha Mitchell, Lourdes Paten-Carver, Paula Patten-McDonald, Lewis M. Riddick Jr. and Marsha Rippy, all Jermantown Cemetery descendants.[77] County court records have the nonprofit registered on March 24, 2015, with the Virginia State Commission Corporation Clerks Information System.[78]

Rita Colbert and niece in School Street area, 1990s. *Photo courtesy of authors.*

Dennis Howard would be the chair of both the nonprofit and the trusteeship. After his death in 2016, the nonprofit lapsed, with a dissolution date of July 31, 2018.[79]

When the COVID pandemic came upon us, local Truro Anglican Church members, as part of a racial unity reconciliation group called RRG, sought opportunities to gather safely in person, to learn and to serve in Fairfax, Virginia. They met with Susan Gray, City of Fairfax historical manager, to better understand local African American history. She told them about Jermantown Cemetery, a neglected historic cemetery within the city limits. Learning about the cemetery, including its origins as a segregated cemetery, inspired the group to lay Christmas wreaths in remembrance, similar to the tradition at nearby Arlington National Cemetery. Within seven weeks of first discussing the idea, a transformative project in service and relationship-building was born.

Fellow church attendees Tony Zipfel, Jeanne Ayivorh, Will Rowe, Tom Prichard, Debbie Lynch and others in the RRG sought to remember and honor those buried in this cemetery.[80] Tony contacted the City of Fairfax managers and learned he must contact the cemetery's descendants for permission. Constance B. Smith was the only contact they had, and she graciously gave permission to the event and each component involved. In this pandemic winter of 2020, it was difficult to connect with others; however, through the work of and information made available from the Fairfax County Cemetery Preservation Association (FCCPA), founded by Mary Lipsey, more cemetery details became known. Many descendants of those buried were affiliated with the local Mount Calvary Baptist Church. Many church buildings were closed during the pandemic, and it would not be until later that connections to the church and family members would be made. At this first remembrance and wreath ceremony for the ancestors, Smith and her son were the only descendants present to recognize family members.

For this special occasion, members of the racial unity reconciliation group (RRG) decided to make homemade pine wreaths. To make the wreaths, acknowledging the serious nature of the pandemic, the group gathered the Saturday before the ceremony in the cold outdoors, on a large driveway. They spread out to create Christmas wreaths with fresh pine boughs, wiring them to the frames with handcrafted Christmas bows. There was much laughter and gratitude for being able to gather safely. No one feared lack of artistic skills. Taking the time to honor and remember is what mattered.

On December 19, 2020, a group of about twenty people gathered for this special wreath-laying and remembrance event at Jermantown Cemetery (south side of Route 50, a quarter-mile mile west of Route 29-211) in Fairfax, Virginia. Special guest speakers included the mayor, David Meyer, and Virginia state senator Chap Petersen. Two RRG members—an army and a marine veteran, respectively—also provided a humbling recognition of the veteran brothers buried at the cemetery. This tradition continues with an additional cemetery ceremony for Juneteenth in the summertime. The Christmas program stated:

In June 2020, a group of diverse Christians from the Fairfax, Virginia area started on a racial unity journey that involves listening and learning

Mayor David Meyer at Christmas wreath-laying ceremony at Jermantown Cemetery, 2022, his last public event before retiring. *Photo courtesy of Jenee Lindner.*

in humility about our nation's racial past and its legacy impact on us today. From educating themselves on history, they began a journey of taking action—to be the change they wish to see continue in the world.

We gather to honor all family relations and ancestors buried at Jermantown Cemetery. We don't know all the names in this hallowed site—but our thoughts are with those who came before us. Although unknown to us, you are known and loved by God.

The late Dennis Howard spoke of the history of African Americans in Fairfax County from the nineteenth century. He provided an oral history which can be found on the www.Braddockheritage.org site. He recreates the story of his own family from slavery to the present day. His ancestor, Horace Gibson, buried at Jermantown Cemetery, and fellow former slave Moses Parker, established a blacksmith shop and purchased land near the intersection of Little River Turnpike and Prosperity Avenue after the Civil War. The partners eventually expanded their holdings to 400 acres, and the area later became known as Ilda, a community of shops and a church likely named after Matilda Gibson Parker, daughter of Horace and daughter-in-law of Moses. [Mr. Howard had been the last active Jermantown Cemetery Trustee Chair.]

We placed each wreath on a gravestone. At the same time, we repeated the name on the gravestone and stood in honor of them for one minute. If no name was there, a minute of honored silence was given. As hoped, it was a very moving experience for those who attended.

When a small seed is planted on good soil, with care and divine sunlight, it will grow. That is exactly what happened. What began as a wreath healing program expanded into more cooperative projects with churches, cemetery descendants and charities.

Soon, cemetery descendants, racial unity members, church sponsors and service groups enthusiastically joined in. An overall purpose of the Jermantown Cemetery plan was laid out, with a vision for the preservation of the cemetery and the numbered steps to get to this vision. Today, some are ongoing, and some have been completed.

1. Work closely with the cemetery trustees and cemetery descendants
2. Reach out to Mount Calvary Baptist Church, especially Reverend Jeffery Johnson
3. Establish a not-for-profit for the cemetery
4. Form a multidisciplinary project team

The early days of creating the Jermantown Cemetery Preservation Society, September 2021. *Left to right*: Kristyne Torruella, Rita Colbert, Linneall Naylor, Inece Bryant, Ron Crittendon (*behind*), Robert MacKay, Will Rowe, Teresa Rowe, Jenee Lindner (*behind*), Matthew Archer-Beck, Adam Bishop, Tom Prichard, Gloria Runyon, DeeDee Carter. *Photo courtesy of Will Rowe.*

5. Establish a formal signage for the cemetery
6. Develop a map of the cemetery with the locations of all markers and gravestones
7. For each ancestor, collect historical information and pictures of each marker, and link all of this to locations on a storyboard map
8. Place and maintain all information on a Jermantown website with search capabilities
9. Provide property maintenance (grass, trees, gravestones)
10. Conduct research and add to the website
11. Conduct outreach to build supportive partnerships[81]

With descendants and likeminded patrons at the helm, a new nonprofit called Jermantown Cemetery Preservation Society was created on October 4, 2021, with board members Ron Crittenden as chair, Linneall Naylor as vice chair and Constance B. Smith as secretary/treasurer—all Jermantown Cemetery descendants.[82] The next year, Linneall Naylor was made chair, Rondia Prescott vice chair, Constance B. Smith secretary/treasurer and Vickie Lucas sergeant-at-arms.

CLEANING UP THE CEMETERY, BY NED FOSTER

On Saturday, November 13, 2021, a group of descendants and volunteers banded together to complete an astonishingly laborious and thorough cleaning of Jermantown Cemetery.[83] Ned Foster wrote for the Fairfax County Cemetery Preservation Society on its Facebook page:

> *They sanded and painted fence railings and cleared out a mountain of plant debris and trash and piled it up for a Fairfax City crew to haul away. The trash…measured is 25' long, 10' wide, and 7' tall.*
>
> *It was no easy task coordinating this work. The young folks were the strength of the overall effort and seemed tireless. The older folks helped too, and a number of them brought gas-powered tools that helped immensely. Despite the cold, much progress was made, including finding more burial sites marked by small stones on the east side under the holly due to the knowledge of family members who helped clear the area. Some think there may be another marker on the southwest side corner too.*

Descendants, church youth and other likeminded people cleaning the Jermantown Cemetery on a gorgeous fall day. *Photo courtesy of Carl Reid.*

Special thanks to Jermantown Preservation Society and The Church of Jesus Christ of Latter-day Saints Young Men and Young Women youth groups and supporting adults. We especially thank the volunteers who are descendants of many of the deceased in Jermantown. Thanks also to the RRG (Racial unity Reconciliation Group), the Fairfax County Cemetery Preservation Association, the stalwart survey/mapping volunteers from Booz Allen Hamilton, and so many families and friends. We had over 40 people there on this one-acre plot to clean and point out graves. Many are not marked anymore. This could not have been done without the support of the eight descendants that came to show us the way and teach us about their worthy ancestors….

Jermantown Cemetery holds a deep abiding history. It is very worthy of being maintained and treasured by all of us.

Below is an excerpt from an article published for Women's Month in our local newspaper above the cemetery's evolution.

Fairfax Woman [Helps] *Form Nonprofit to Preserve Jermantown Cemetery: Smith Works to Revitalize Neglected Grounds*
By Jaya Patil, Fairfax County Times
Updated March 23, 2022

The Jermantown Cemetery has been officially established since 1868 but was the unofficial burial site for African Americans for far longer. For Constance "Connie" Smith, Jermantown Cemetery is the resting place for generations of family. Smith brought the cemetery from a neglected plot of land to revitalized grounds over the last few years.

Benevolent societies, which start the story, existed since the Civil War for the sake of supporting African American communities. The cemetery was created when the Burial Sons and Daughters of Benevolence of Fairfax Court House purchased an acre of land for proper burial of their dead.

Smith's roots with the cemetery run deep, as her great-grandfather Lewis Jackson was a part of that founding society. She has attended burials at the cemetery since the age of five. Smith lost her mother when she was nine and her custodial aunt at 13. At the burials as a child, she said, "I remember feeling perplexed, like there should be something that says their names… [and wondering why] *they don't have headstones." Smith later learned of the racism behind the absence of headstones in cemeteries for African Americans and decided she would mark the graves of her family one day.*

The trustees of the founding society all passed away without appointing successors, so ownership of the cemetery remains undetermined. Fairfax [City] took over minimal upkeep of the cemetery. After three children and 13 years as an Arlington County Government administrative professional, Smith retired in 2013 and felt the opportunity to revisit her goal.

Smith got in contact with Historian Mary Lipsey when she asked to put a grave marker down for her family in 2014. A flat marble stone engraved with the names of her family members now marks their burial location. Although, the fear of disinterment plagued her, as she said, "I was afraid that one day I would go up there and [the graves] just wouldn't be there."…

Smith mused, "My mother died when I was nine, I knew her for nine years. Somehow it feels like, by doing this, she's there with me—the family is with me."[84]

On June 23, 2023, a new trusteeship was created on behalf of the Jermantown Cemetery Preservation Society, called the Jermantown Cemetery Trusteeship. It was approved by Fairfax County Circuit Court judge Grace Burke Carroll, with new trustees Dayna Burns, Linneall Naylor, Vickie Lucas, Rita Colbert and Rondia Prescott, all cemetery descendants.[85] They thank the former trustees for all their service, including Shakira Howard, the last trustee under her father's leadership.

JERMANTOWN CEMETERY SURVEY

Jermantown Cemetery is located at 11085 Fairfax Boulevard, Fairfax, Virginia 22030. Before 1860, the law said the enslaved were not allowed to learn to read and write. Even if they could read and write, they would not mark a grave with the deceased's name and date, for fear of reprisal. Fieldstones and wooden crosses handmade by African American families and friends marked their graves. This was done in almost all African American cemeteries in Virginia and across the South.[86] Fieldstones were found in Jermantown Cemetery, still visible. Partly because of this evidence and evidence of enslaved quarters for Richard Ratcliffe's Mount Vineyard Plantation next to it, it is believed it was a graveyard for servants and the enslaved for many years before it was formally created in 1868 after the American Civil War and named Jermantown Cemetery.[87]

Overhead map of Jermantown Cemetery, Fairfax, Virginia, with outline of one-acre site. Route 50, Fairfax Boulevard (Little River Turnpike) is on the right. Route 29 (Warrenton Turnpike) is on the left. *Photo courtesy of Sam Lindner.*

The Jermantown Cemetery Fairfax County Circuit Court Land Deed describes the cemetery as being "a certain piece or parcel of [land]…lying on the Little River Turnpike about one mile west of Fairfax Court House… to make one acre."[88]

There are fifty-four stone or metal markers still on-site, with a few scattered fieldstones. The last person was buried there in the early 1990s, and the cemetery was then considered filled by descendants. Family descendants have been making a carefully crafted new grave list with the help of other historians and their own research, including Etta Willson, Linneall Naylor, Rita Colbert, Rondia Prescott and Jenee Lindner. The grave list of around 180 ancestors in the following pages reflects all the verified information thus far. There is more work to do.

A ground penetration radar survey was recently completed in cooperation with volunteers at Booz Allen Hamilton Corp. and Jason Boroughs, research archaeologist, George Washington's Mount Vernon. The survey found 138 graves—depressions—in the soil. We know that sometimes people, especially couples, will have caskets one on top of the other to conserve family space (even today this is done). That makes the total number of those buried at the Jermantown Cemetery likely higher.

Left: Row of Harris family tombstones. Dr. Jason Burroughs came with several George Washington University students to do a study of the underground area. Using a ground-penetrating radar (GPR) machine, they crossed the cemetery in grids to map out precisely where the graves were located. *Photo courtesy of Jenee Lindner.*

Below: Tombstone row of Harris family above Jemantown Cemetery *Photo courtesy of Jason Burroughs, PhD, RPA research archaeologist, George Washington's Mount Vernon.*

Opposite: Row of Harris family tombstones. Ground-penetrating radar (GPR) was used to see if there were more graves underneath or manmade disturbances indicating grave shafts not observed above the ground. They were still intact and followed the row of tombstones. It all appeared fine. The team of investigators found several other rows of graves that were not marked as prominently. *Photo courtesy of Dr. Jason Burroughs, with permission from the Harris family.*

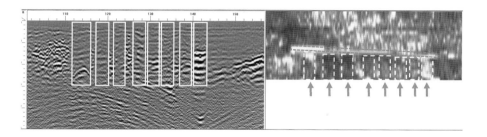

JERMANTOWN CEMETERY SURVEY LIST

NAME	BORN	DIED	
Allen, Fontaine Isabel	7-29-1925	8-13-1925	Daughter of Phillip/ Virginia Payne Allen
Anderson, Catherine Idella Johnson	10-4-1865	11-15-1994	Wife of John Luther Anderson
Anderson, Isabella Groomes	1889	1918	Wife of Frank Anderson
Anderson, John	1887	Not legible	Husband of Laura Anderson, within iron fence
Anderson, Laura M.	1888	1965	Wife of John Anderson, within iron fence
Anderson, Silas Edward (Buddy)	6-7-1873		Parents: George Anderson Sr./Elizabeth Anderson Husband of Adelaide M. Lomax (birth about 1879)
Anderson, Wilson R.	1911	1962	Son of John/Laura Anderson, within iron fence
Ball, Carrie		11-3-1933	Daughter of William Ball
Ball, Carrie Smith	1860	10-10-1933	Wife of Thomas Ball
Bernaugh/Burnaugh, Charles			Husband of Nancy Nelson Bernaugh
Bernaugh, Daniel	1863	1913	Husband of Lutricia
Bernaugh, Nancy Nelson	1846	12-20-1929	Wife of Charles Bernaugh; Father: Thomas Nelson; Mother: Ella Gales Sister: Lutricia

NAME	BORN	DIED	
Bowles, Agnes	5-22-1923	1-16-1963	Daughter of Walter/Susie Bowles
Bowles, Daniel		Bef. 1929	Husband of Susie Bowles. Father of Walter
Bowles, Daniel	1858	1929	Husband of Roberta Hampton
Bowles, Susie		2-22-1929	Wife of Daniel Bowles. Mother of Walter
Bowles, Robert	1854	1915	
Bowles, Roberta Hampton	1858	2-16-1929	Wife of Daniel Bowles
Bowles, Walter	12-4-1925	11-2-1932	Son of Daniel/Susie Bowles
Brooks, Agnes	1812	5-9-1872	Wife of Milton George Brooks, two daughters
Brooks, James Atwood	1-5-1927	8-17-1931	Son of James E. Brooks/Mary Payne Brooks
Brooks, James Emanuel	2-1-1906	2-19-1955	Son of Frank/Isabel Brooks. Husband of Mary Payne Brooks
Brooks, Milton George	1809	1896	Father of Margaret B. Gibson/Eveline B. Murray
Butler, Belle		10-16-1923	Daughter of Adam Cleveland/Belle Wheeler. Wife of George Butler
Carter, Thomas	12-15-1918	3-17-1963	Son of Thomas Carter/Ada Murray
Chambers, Daniel			
Chambers, Georgia A.	9-29-1894	5-26-1961	
Chambers, Lillie Osceola	1897	1954	Wife of Richard Daniel Chambers (Veteran)
Chambers, Margaret (Maggie)		1933	Wife of Luther Chambers
Chambers, William J.	9-16-1886	7-18-1955	Husband of Georgia Chambers
Clarke, Mary		12-14-1928	Wife of Will Clarke

To the Memory of Mrs. Agnes Brooks Born 1812
Died May 1872. Jermantown Cemetery, Fairfax,
Virginia. *Photo courtesy of Jenee Lindner.*

NAME	BORN	DIED	
Clarke, Will		Aft. 1928	Husband of Mary Clarke
Colbert, Anderson	1895	1897	Son of Jacob C. Colbert/ Martha H. Colbert
Colbert, Andrew	1897	1897	Son of Jacob C. Colbert/ Martha H. Colbert
Colbert, Annie M.	1887	1887	Daughter of Jacob C. Colbert/Martha H. Colbert
Colbert, Clarence Washington	2-9-1898	12-15-1960	Son of Jacob C. Colbert/ Martha H. Colbert
Colbert, infant girl	1954	1954	Daughter of Dorsey/ Delores Colbert
Colbert, Jacob C.	1854	6-17-1935	Husband of Martha H. Colbert. Son of Isaac/ Louisa
Colbert, Jacob Buchanan (Buck)	1889	1940	Son of Jacob C. Colbert/ Martha H. Colbert
Colbert, Mary Elizabeth Butler	1888	5-19-1962	Daughter of George/ Mary Wheeler Butler. Wife of Jacob B. Colbert
Colbert, Mary L. Green	2-19-1900	10-21-1961	Wife of Clarence Colbert
Colbert, Martha (Mollie) Helen Young	1857	7-10-1935	Wife of Jacob C. Colbert

NAME	BORN	DIED	
Colbert, William Andrew	1891	1893	Son of Jacob C. Colbert/ Martha H. Colbert
Conic, Carrie L.	5-14-1874	2-16-1956	Wife of William Henry Conic
Conic, William H.	1869	1943	Husband of Carrie L. Conic
Dixon, Margaret			
Dotson, William Marshall	6-15-1885	12-20-1951	Husband of Liza
Felton, Harriett Johnson Conic	1844	4-2-1921	Wife of Isaac Felton/ Simon Peter Conic
Ford, Benjamin	1-15-1895	11-21-1943	Husband of Lottie Murray Ford
Ford, Georgeanna Turner	8-30-1861	2-24-1943	Wife of Robert Ford
Ford, Lottie	1881	1981	Wife of Benjamin Ford
Gibson, Brooks E.	6-12-1862	1-19-1897	Husband of Minta Banks
Gibson, Eveline/Everline	7-12-1876		
Gibson, Horace	4-15-1817	4-27-1912	Husband of Margaret Brooks Gibson
Gibson, Margaret Brooks	1-1-1827	1-15-1911	Wife of Horace Gibson
Gibson, Martha Weir	1-1-1845	10-18-1926	Wife of Strother Gibson
Gibson, Strother	4-13-1846	4-16-1927	Husband of Martha Weir Gibson
Gibson, Thomas	1-1874	4-8-1874	Son of Horace and Margaret Gibson
Gray, Martha Ellen Lucas	12-29-1880	2-15-1946	Wife of Ernest Gray
Gray, Ernest	1880	1946	Husband of Martha Ellen Lucas Gray
Groomes, Bradshaw	1885	1947	Husband of Martha Gibson Groomes
Groomes, Lizzie		5-3-1918	Daughter of John Groomes
Groomes, Martha Gibson	1889	1949	Wife of Bradshaw Groomes
Grooms/Groomes, Isabella Snowden	9-23-1857	9-23-1917	Daughter of John Snowden and Amanda Pollard

Jermantown Cemetery. *Photo courtesy of Jenee Lindner.*

NAME	BORN	DIED	
Harris, Alphonso	8-22-1902	12-27-1968	
Harris, Corinthia	1847	7-6-1927	Within iron fence, three stones illegible but identified
Harris, James A., private, USMC	10-13-1930	12-21-1973	Husband of Phyllis Allen Harris
Harris, Virginia M.	11-19-1908	9-1-1989	Wife of Alphonso Harris
Harris, Maurice Watson	2-10-1928	6-12-1991	Corporal, U.S. Army, Korea. Son of Alphonso/ Virginia
Harris-Minor, Sylvia Louise	10-28-1935	8-24-1980	Daughter of Alphonso/ Virginia Harris
Harrod, Dorothea Strother Groomes	01-28-1919	11-21-1977	Wife of Franklin H. Harrod Parents: Bradshaw/ Martha Gibson Groomes
Harrod, Franklin Howard	11-4-1922	1-22-1960	Parents: Joseph P./Susie Brown Harrod. Husband of Dorothea Groomes Harrod. Son-in-law of Bradshaw and Martha Groomes
Hedgemon, Martha Colbert	1894	1952	Wife of William D. Hedgemon

NAME	BORN	DIED	
Hedgemon, William D.	1885	1946	Husband of Martha Colbert Hedgemon
Hunter, George	1891	1947	Son of Robert/Margaret Morarity Hunter
Hunter, Henry	1871	1893	Son of Charles and Caroline Hunter
Hunter, James K.			Husband of Sarah Jane Neale Whaley
Hunter, Margaret Elizabeth Turley	9-17-1855	10-29-1912	Wife of Robert Hunter
Hunter, Robert	1855	1926	Husband of Margaret (Maggie) Hunter
Hunter, Ruth Anderson	5-15-1897	3-4-1933	Wife of George Thomas Hunter
Jackson, Ada C. Bell	July 1889	Not legible	
Jackson, Celenia			Mother of Lewis E. Jackson. Wife of Lewis Jackson
Jackson, Ernest Eugene	1924	1983	Son of Raymond/Hattie Jackson
Jackson, Harold Kiah	1922	1982	Son of Raymond/Hattie Jackson
Jackson, Hattie Kiah	1883	1952	Wife of Raymond Jackson
Jackson, Henry			Husband of Lucy/Lucie Richards Jackson
Jackson, Lewis			Father of Lewis E. Jackson. Husband of Celenia
Jackson, Lewis E.		12-22-1929	Son of Lewis/Celenia Jackson
Jackson, Lucy/Lucie Richards			Wife of Henry Jackson
Jackson, Malvina	1844	5-3-1919	Wife of Lewis E. Jackson
Jackson, Raymond Lewis	1881	1964	Husband of Hattie Kye
Jackson, William Lewis	1919	1920	Son of Raymond/Hattie Jackson

NAME	BORN	DIED	
Johnson, Mabel A.	1898	1965	
Johnson, Walter P.	12-20-1897	12-9-1978	Husband of Amy Johnson
Jones, Amber Alice Dodson	10-31-1882	5-5-1967	Wife of George Jones
Lamb, George	1834	1926	
Lucas, Lucinda	1851	1-27-1933	Sister of Nancy Burnage, two daughters/sons
Marshall, Ella Colbert	1887	1976	Wife of Frank Marshall. Daughter of Jacob/ Martha Colbert
Marshall, Frank J.	1886	1929	Husband of Ella Colbert Marshall
Martin, John W.	10-25-1883	3-22-1976	
Martin, Sylvia	1883	1940	
Martin, William R.	5-9-1915	10-20-1954	
McConico, Avelina Suggs		10-8-1950	
McConico, Sidney	1873	4-10-1951	Husband of Evalina McConico
Melontree, Martin		1917	Son of Isaac Melontree. Husband of Patsy Elizabeth Young
Money, Wilmer Edward	10-7-1903	1-10-1951	Son of Adeline Gunter.
Morarity, Della Turner	1859	9-9-1926	Wife of Joseph Morarity
Morarity, Horace	10-14-1898	5-15-1926	Husband of Ceola Hampton
Morarity, Louvenia	2-12-1880	7-18-1949	Mother of Mabel, Victor, Warren, Louis, Lloyd
Morarity, Thomas	11-27-1864	12-1-1944	Husband of Louvenia Morarity
Morarity, Victor Warren	12-2-1895	4-1-1968	Husband of Elizabeth Morarity
Murray, Eveline Brooks	1849	11-19-1927	Wife of Joshua Murray
Murray, George Percy	4-1899	8-1-1962	Husband of Isabella Murray

Jermantown Cemetery. *Photo courtesy of Jenee Lindner.*

NAME	BORN	DIED	
Murray, Joshua Ray, Sr.	1865	1910	Husband of Eveline B. Murray. Father of Josh Ray
Murray, Joshua Ray, Jr.	1884	1927	Husband of Malinda Murray
Murray, Laura	7-15-1898	5-23-1945	Daughter of Joshua and Celine Murray
Murray, Malinda S.	1894	1-28-1927	Wife of Joshua Ray Murray
Neale, Amy	1830	3-13-1911	Wife of Henry Neale
Neale, Henry	1835	1919	Husband of Amy Neale
Nickens, Hester	1851	1921	Wife of Hezekiah Nickens
Nickens, Hezekiah	1838	8-22-1911	Husband of Hester Nickens
Oliver, Louise Gibson	8-28-1870	4-7-1950	Daughter of Strother Gibson/Martha Davis
Parks, Ethel Elizabeth Jackson	1914	1960	Daughter of Raymond/ Hattie Jackson
Payne, Antonia Hunter	7-14-1877	5-27-1939	Wife of Robert (Bob) Payne
Payne, Benjamin, Sr.	1867	1950	Husband of Martha Tibbs Payne
Payne, Charity Tibbs	1863	1942	Wife of Washington Payne Sr. Sister of Martha Tibbs Payne

NAME	BORN	DIED	
Payne, Charlie	6-2-1881	4-28-1959	Son of Washington W. Payne/Charity Tibbs Payne
Payne, Eastern	4-19-1899	10-9-1950	Husband of Margaret A. Payne, Sarah Conic Payne
Payne, Hazel J.	1928	1933	Daughter of Leonard Bowles Payne/Viola Bowles Payne
Payne, James Robert	11-19-1919	11-16-1922	Son of Eastern Payne/Sarah Conic Payne
Payne, Lewis, Jr.	1860	12-22-1947	Husband of Molly Payne
Payne, Lewis, Sr.	1820	Bef. 1900	Husband of Malinda Ford Payne
Payne, Malinda Ford	1829	1-8-1920	Wife of Lewis Payne Sr.
Payne, Martha Tibbs	1872	7-31-1926	Wife of Reverend Benjamin F. Payne Sr.
Payne, Sandra Mae	1950	1951	Daughter of Willis Payne/Phyllis Vincent Payne
Payne, Sarah Jane Conic	12-10-1900	11-4-1936	Wife of Eastern Payne
Payne, Washington			Young man, died in accidental shooting
Payne, Washington W., Sr.	1854	4-6-1938	Husband of Charity Tibbs Payne
Payne, Washington P., Jr.	7-4-1890	2-18-1962	Husband of Alice L. Payne
Payton, Maggie	1895	1938	
Pearson, Darber		Aft. 1887	
Perry, Lulu	1882	1918	Wife of Wade Perry
Perry, Rosia	12-1907	1-8-1919	Daughter of Wade and Lulu Perry
Perry, Wade	3-15-1854	5-19-1934	Husband of Lulu Ashton/Susana Johnson
Perry, Warner	1900	12-31-1918	Son of Wade Perry and Lulu Ashton
Pinkett, Mary Payne	1856	11-20-1937	First husband: Jack Selvie. Second husband: Edward Pinkett

NAME	BORN	DIED	
Pleasant, Ada C. Bell Jackson		1889	Wife of Samuel Pleasant
Richards, Nancy			
Runner, Benjamin	1849	7-28-1915	Husband of Jane Runner
Runner, Jane	1850	12-16-1910	Wife of Benjamin Runner
Runner, Sarah Ellen	1854	10-8-1897	Wife of Winfield Runner
Runner, Winfield	1854	1910	Husband of Sarah Ellen Runner
Simms, Lewis	Jan. 1830	Bef. 1920	Husband of Martha Simms
Simms, Martha (Patsy)	June 1825	1925	Wife of Lewis Simms
Sinkfield, Thomas W.	1823	9-30-1896	Husband of Mary Sinkfield
Sinkfield, Mary Ellen Murphy		1831	
Smith, Dorothy Belle Jackson	1916	1957	Daughter of Raymond/ Hattie Jackson
Spriggs, Addie	1862	4-26-1911	Widow
Tibbs, Patsy Elizabeth	3-18-1849	7-18-1928	Husband of Jesse Melontree. Second husband: Solomon Tibbs. Sister of Martha (Mollie) Helen Young Colbert
Tibbs, Solomon, Jr.	1854	10-26-1915	Husband of Patsy Young
Turner, Henson	1853	7-4-1924	Husband of Mary Turner, Brother of Della Morarity
Whaley, Alfred	1830	11-22-1891	Husband of Matilda Whaley
Whaley, John R.		7-3-1872	Son of Alfred/Matilda, killed by wagon
Whaley, Matilda	1828	1905	Wife of Alfred Whaley
Whiting, Thomas	1842	1-6-1916	Husband of Jennie
Winston, Russell	10-18-1913	6-26-1956	Husband of Hilda Marshall Winston

Chapter 3

DESCENDANTS REMEMBER

THEIR ANCESTORS

On February 28, 2022, for Black History Month, Virginia senator Chap Petersen spoke before the Virginia State Assembly about the contributions Reverend Benjamin Franklin Payne made to the Fairfax City community. He also spoke of Reverend Payne's son Atana Payne, whom he knew, and the Jermantown Cemetery.[89]

REVEREND BENJAMIN FRANKLIN PAYNE (1867–1950)

by Etta Willson, Granddaughter

I have only a vague memory of my maternal grandfather, Reverend Benjamin Franklin Payne, because he died when I was six years old. As a young child, I heard many stories about him from my mother and other relatives. He was called PaPa by his children and grandchildren and was affectionately called Uncle Benny by his nieces, nephews and close family friends. My grandfather was born on December 31, 1867, in Locustdale, Madison County, Virginia, four years after the Emancipation Proclamation was signed. His parents were Lewis and Malinda (Ford) Payne, who had been enslaved. In 1886, his father, Lewis, purchased a quarter of an acre of land located at Ox Hill and Little River Turnpike Road and migrated his family to the area. The area was called Pender at the time and is now

Above: Payne family reunion, summer 2022. *Story board courtesy of Rita Colbert, Dayna Burns and Rondia Prescott. Photo courtesy of Jenee Lindner.*

Opposite: Virginia senator Chap Petersen and Reverend Jeffrey Johnson at Jermantown Cemetery event, 2021. *Photo courtesy of Jenee Lindner.*

referred to as the Fair Oaks area of Fairfax. Benjamin grew up working on the farm with his siblings.

Reverend Payne's wife was Martha Tibbs, who was born in 1872 in Fauquier County, Virginia. They were married on November 20, 1888, in Washington, D.C. In 1896, they purchased five acres of land with a large farmhouse. The land was located on Legato Road in Fairfax near what is now Fair Oaks Mall. They were blessed with nine children: Richard, Clarence, Benjamin Jr., Leonard, Simon Atana, Eastern, John, Antonia Virginia and Mary. Benjamin and Martha reared their children in the reverential fear and knowledge of God. There are memories of Benjamin sitting with a Bible in his lap reading the word of God to his children and grandchildren.

Martha maintained the household and cooked for her large family. The daughters rose early before school to help with the cooking. The male family members helped on the farm. They attended the school located near Fairfax County Courthouse, which had been established for African American students in the 1870s.

Benjamin was ordained as a Baptist minister in 1920 at Mt. Calvary Baptist Church, Fairfax, Virginia, under the leadership of the first pastor, Reverend Marshall D. Williams. Mt. Calvary Baptist Church is still active and is now located at 4325 Chain Bridge Road, Fairfax, Virginia. My grandfather was a well-respected and esteemed citizen of the county, as noted in a *Washington Bee* newspaper article dated June 3, 1916. He was appointed chaplain of the Fairfax Colored School League. He also performed wedding ceremonies for family members and friends.

Reverend Benjamin Franklin Payne. *Photo courtesy of Etta Willson.*

Reverend Payne held church services in his home, where Martha served dinner and homemade ice cream to her guests. They had a farm in Legato, the next town over from Jermantown. The story has been passed down by family members that Martha had a beautiful voice and, while driving up the long driveway to their home, one could hear her singing hymns along with the family. They praised God a capella and with hand clapping and foot stomping to keep the rhythm. That was church! It was a simpler time—a time of family gatherings that taught the importance of a strong faith in God and family cohesiveness and support.

The photographer of the picture opposite wrote in August 1914:

> *It is a rough road the Warrenton Turnpike and Route 29* [but] *before the war was one of the finest roads of the country. It was 50 feet wide, hard and fairly smooth, but hilly. Now it is one of the worst. After the incoming of railroads, it was somewhat neglected. During the Civil War it was altogether neglected so far as repairs were concerned and was pounded and rutted and worn out and gullied by the army* [wagon] *trains—artillery quartermaster and commissary—for four years. In a dip between hills, you pass a little village strung along both sides of the road. It has the curious name of Legato, with this stress on the second syllable. It used to be famous for a distillery not operated now though the old building remains. Ridge after ridge and valley you cross for seven Virginia miles out of Fairfax and a mile before you reach the end of your walk you see a cluster of houses perched on high land. That's Centerville.*[90]

Reverend Payne was eventually called to pastor the Mt. Olive Baptist Church in Centerville, Virginia, where he served from the late 1930s until 1948. He also served as pastor at the Prosperity Baptist Church in Chantilly and at the Dean Divers Baptist Church in Manassas, Virginia. He was often

The Legato area, next to Jermantown, was home to the Payne family farm. *From* This Was Virginia 1900–1927 as Shown by Glass Negatives of J. Harry Shannon, the Rambler, *compiled by Connie and Mayo Stuntz. Courtesy of the Virginia Room, Fairfax County Public Library.*

accompanied by family members who provided the music for his services. Martha died in 1926 in Washington, D.C., and Benjamin died in 1950 in Washington, D.C. Both are buried at the Historical Jermantown Cemetery, Fairfax, Virginia.

My grandfather's legacy continues, as many of his descendants faithfully serve and worship God at Mt. Calvary and other churches. Many of us have passed on or moved away, but the memories remain in our hearts, and the story continues.

ELLA COLBERT MARSHALL (1887–1976)

By Brenda Duncan, Granddaughter

Ella Colbert Marshall was daughter of Martha Young Colbert and Jacob Colbert. She was born on July 23, 1887, in Loudoun County. When she was young, her family moved to Fairfax County to the Jermantown community,

Ella Colbert Marshall. *Courtesy of Brenda Duncan.*

a mile and a half west of downtown Fairfax City, Virginia. She attended a one-room schoolhouse "set back on the hill between the cemetery and the undertaker's shop off Main Street." According to Ella in a taped interview, "There was an old wood-burning stove that sat in the middle of the floor. Just one teacher who taught there for years and years. His name was Roberts. And there was an old outhouse, of course." Grades 1 through 6 were taught in this school.

In speaking of her youth, Ella said, "I guess life was harder for people back then, but for us it was easy because we didn't know any other life. Of course, my father usually did work he could contract, like cutting a field of corn for so much. There were mostly corn and wheat fields around here then, and my brother and I would go and help him."

Ella married Frank Marshall of Culpeper, Virginia, and together they owned and operated a general store at the corner of Payne (now Highway 123) and School Street in Fairfax. They lived in five rooms in the back of a two-story structure, which housed a dance hall and barbershop on the second floor. It was here their first three children were born: Hilda Marshall Tillery, Mary Frances Marshall Reed and Archie Colbert Marshall. Later, the family moved to 10629 West Drive in Fairfax, where Evelyn Marshall Murphy and Helen Marshall Walker were born. Mrs. Marshall continued to live in the house her husband had built on West Drive until her death.

Mrs. Marshall often spoke of the many times she and her husband extended credit to not only Black families but also some of the poor White families who lived in the community. Although many of these customers never paid anything on their bills at the store, Mrs. Marshall continued this practice of not refusing anyone really in need during the short time she ran the store alone after her husband's death in 1929.

Following a brief illness, Mrs. Marshall passed away on November 16, 1976, and is buried beside her husband in Jermantown Cemetery, Fairfax, Virginia.

JACOB C. COLBERT (1854–1935)

by Rita Colbert and Rondia Prescott

COLBERT, JACOB C. On Monday, June 17, 1935, at 8:40 p.m., at his residence, Fairfax, Va., JACOB C. COLBERT, beloved husband of Martha H. Colbert and father of Ella Colbert Marshall. Jacob C. Colbert, Martha H. Hedgemon and Clarence W. Colbert. Funeral will be held from his late residence on Wednesday, June 19, at 3 p.m., Rev. B. F. Payne officiating. Interment in family burial ground, Germantown, Va.

Evening Star newspaper, June 18, 1935.
Courtesy of Rondia Prescott.

Jacob C. Colbert was born and raised in Oatlands, Loudoun County, Virginia. At present we are unsure of Jacob's beginnings, but we would like to share his legacy.

Jacob would find love with his first wife, Agness Champ, in 1881. She would birth his first son, Samuel Colbert. Tragically, Agness and Samuel would perish in 1884 of consumption.

Jacob would find love again with Martha "Mollie" Helen Young. They were married on August 12, 1885, in Mercer, Loudoun County, Virginia. There, he owned land and farmed for a living. I'm not sure what brought him to Fairfax City. However, he would own property, own a business and register to vote. Mollie would go on to have nine children, only five would live to be adults.

LIST OF SOME OF THE COLBERTS RESTING IN JERMANTOWN CEMETERY

Jacob C. Colbert (1854–1935)
His wife, Martha Helen Young-Colbert (1857–1935)
Their children:
    Annie M. Colbert (1887–1887)
    Ella B. Colbert-Marshall (1887–1976)
    Ella's husband, Frank J. Marshall (1885–1929)
    Jacob Buchannan "Buck" Colbert (1889–1940)
    Jacob's wife, Mary Elizabeth Butler-Colbert (1888–1962)
    William Andrew Colbert (1891–1893)
    Martha Helen Colbert-Hedgemon (1894–1952)
    Martha's husband, William D. Hedgemon (1885–1946)
    Anderson Colbert (1895–1895)
    Andrew Colbert (1897–1897)
    Clarence Washington Colbert (1898–1960)

Right: Mary Butler Colbert, Rita Colbert's grandmother, wife of Jacob B. Colbert; both Mary and Jacob are buried in Jermantown Cemetery. *Photo courtesy of Rita Colbert.*

Below: Rondia Prescott and her son Titus Prescott helping clean up the Jermantown Cemetery, home of their ancestors. *Photo courtesy of Jenee Lindner.*

MARTHA GIBSON GROOMES (1885–1949)
AND FRANKLIN HOWARD HARROD (1922–1960)

by Jenee Lindner, from notes by DeeDee Carter

DeeDee Carter, Jermantown Cemetery descendant, showed the grave-marking crew led by Will Rowe some depressions of grave sites that had been missed once foliage was removed back in the fall of 2021. These are her ancestors.

The two beautiful stone markers were intact, with soil depressions indicating other graves surrounding them. The markers are for Martha G. Groomes, wife of Bradshaw Groomes, and her son-in-law Franklin H. Harrod, who married her daughter Doretha. DeeDee Carter said there were other Groomes and Harrod families who intermarried and are buried in Jermantown Cemetery, but their graves are no longer marked. Besides here, there are many other interconnected families of hers like the Carter family who are buried in neighboring Vienna, Virginia. An article was written about them in 2022; it is excerpted on the following page.

Left: Martha G. Groomes. Jermantown Cemetery. *Photo courtesy of Jenee Lindner.*

Right: Frank H. Harrod. Jermantown Cemetery. *Photo courtesy of Jenee Lindner.*

[Carter] *Family's History in Vienna Spans 160+ Years*
By Michael Marrow, Fairfax County Times
February 25, 2022; updated March 7, 2022

DeArmond, or "DeeDee" Carter, like much of her family, has only known Vienna as her home.

Carter was born and raised there, and her ancestry stretches back generations: Carter has Native American ancestors, and for more than 160 years, the Carter family has owned property in the same area of Vienna, a large tract of land known as the Carter Farm.

It was established in 1859 by Carter's direct ancestors and endured hardships like the Civil War, where soldiers ransacked the property and stole livestock. "They took about everything," Carter said. After the war, her grandfather was only able to reclaim a nominal reimbursement for the damages. She now plans to seek full redress of what was owed.

The family property then passed through descendants. Carter's great grandfather, grandfather, father, and herself all grew up in the same area, which is now located on Courthouse Road. The Carter family contributed much to the growth of the town and was well-known by local residents. One of her ancestors, Lucy Carter, even served as a spy during the Civil War to aid the Union war effort.[91]

LEWIS PAYNE (1820–BEFORE 1900) AND MALINDA FORD PAYNE (1829–1920)

by Linneall Naylor

My name is Linneall Naylor, and I am a descendant of the Jermantown Cemetery burial community. Our known ancestors that are physically resting at Jermantown are Lewis Payne; Malinda Payne; Agnes Brooks; Milton Brooks; Eveline Murray; Josh Murray; Malinda Murray; Joshua Ray Murray, husband of Malinda Murray—and there are many others.

Both Lewis and Malinda were enslaved in Madison County, Virginia, until the 1860s. Our Payne ancestors came to Fairfax County sometime after 1870. In the 1870 census, the Payne family—misspelled "Paino"—were living in Locustdale, Madison County, Virginia. The 1870 census listed the following names: Peter Paino/Payne, born 1790; Lewis Payne, born 1820; Malinda Payne, born 1829 (wife of Lewis Payne); Robert Payne, born

Family of Lewis and Malinda Ford Payne. *Photo and census information courtesy of Linneall Naylor.*

1852; Lucinda Payne, born 1854; Mary Payne, born 1856 (great-great-grandmother), Washington Payne, born 1856; and Lewis Payne, born 1860.

Lewis's eighty-year-old father, Peter Payne (I), is listed in the 1870 census as a farm laborer and mulatto with his son Lewis. Peter Payne (I) was also the

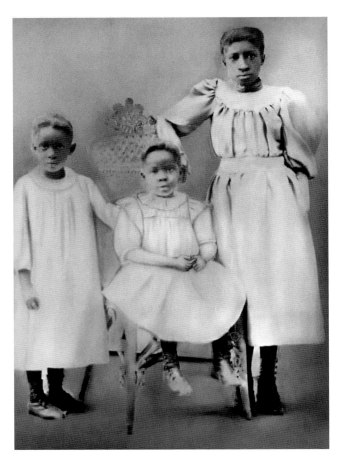

"This is a picture of Lewis and Malinda Payne's children. The earlier picture of Malinda and Lewis, as well as the girls, was owned by the family of Leonard Payne. Leonard's daughter remembers who Lewis and Malinda are in the picture but can't remember who the girls are. This was told to me by Ollie Mae's daughter, a granddaughter of Leonard Payne, Lucinda Marshall." *Rita Colbert.*

father of a son who shared his name, Peter Payne (II). He was born in 1849, and his death certificate is dated July 15, 1921. Peter (II) had parents listed as Peter Payne (I) and Jane Elsy/Ellzey. Jane Ellzey may have been enslaved on the Ellzey plantation located in Fairfax County. Peter Payne (II) is listed in Clifton, Virginia, under the enslavement of Marmaduke Beckwith until his progeny was freed after the Civil War. Lewis Payne died before his wife in Fairfax City, Virginia. Malinda Payne would die on January 8, 1920, in Fairfax City, Virginia.

For my direct line, one of the daughters of Lewis and Malinda Ford Payne (great-great-great grandparents), Mary Payne (great-great grandmother), married John Selvie on October 10, 1878. They had three children: Lewis, Frank and Malinda. Mary Payne Selvie (grandmother) married Edward Pinkett in 1900 after the death of her first husband, Jack Selvie. She worked for the McCandlish family for more than ten years at the Moore house in Fairfax City, Virginia, and died on November 20, 1937. Mary (Payne) Selvie Pinkett is buried at the Jermantown Cemetery.

Malinda (Selvie) Murray (paternal great grandmother) was born in 1887. She was a wife, mother and dressmaker. Malinda Murray died in January 1927 and is buried at Jermantown Cemetery with our ancestors, as well. Joshua Ray Murray (great grandfather) was born on March 4, 1884; died on November 28, 1927; and was buried at Jermantown Cemetery, per his Virginia death notice.

Milton George Brooks, Agnes Brooks, Eveline (Brooks) Murray and Josh Murray all are directly related through DNA/marriages and were instrumental in the establishment of the Jermantown Cemetery in 1868. One reason we do not have a maiden name for Agnes—Brooks is her married name—is because, we believe, she was born enslaved on the Ratcliffe property. Most often, the enslaved were not given a last name. Agnes was a mulatto. Therefore, one of the Ratcliffe family descendants may have been her father, giving her the maiden name of Ratcliffe.

Agnes Brooks (great-great-great grandmother) was born in 1812 and died on May 9, 1872; her burial site is the Jermantown Cemetery. Eveline (Brooks) Murray, daughter of Agnes Brooks, was born in 1849 and died on November 19, 1927; her burial site is the Jermantown Cemetery. This is my direct line.

As a descendant of the Jermantown Cemetery community, I am responsible for reviving our ancestors' lives and existences through the sharing of their ancestral stories by inspiring the next generations of descendants.

My ancestor and great-great grandmother Malinda Murray is buried at Jermantown Cemetery. However, she doesn't have a tombstone or any other known burial identification. Which is why it's so important to me and others to "say their names."

RAYMOND LEWIS JACKSON (1881–1964)
MATERNAL GRANDFATHER OF CONSTANCE B. SMITH

By Constance B. Smith

My maternal grandfather—or "grandpapa," as I called him—was Raymond Lewis Jackson. He was born on April 29, 1881, in Providence, Fairfax, Virginia, and died in Arlington, Virginia, on May 8, 1964. He was married to Hattie Kye, who was also born in Fairfax, Virginia, on December 25, 1883, and who died on April 22, 1952, in Arlington. They had six children, whose names were Thelma Mae, Ethel Elizabeth, Dorothy Belle, William Lewis, Ernest Eugene and Harold Kye. All are buried in the Jermantown Cemetery in Fairfax, Virginia, except for Thelma Mae, who is buried in the Pleasant Valley Cemetery in Annandale, Virginia.

Raymond's parents were Lewis E. Jackson and Malvina Lomax. His father, Lewis, was a member of the colored Lodge No. 4 Burial Sons and Daughters of the Benevolence of Fairfax County. Jermantown Cemetery was deeded to trustees of the Lodge to bury their dead.

Raymond Lewis Jackson. *Photo courtesy of Constance B. Smith.*

Raymond's siblings were Tobias, Ernest, Osie and Alice.

Raymond and his wife and children moved from Fairfax to Arlington in the 1930s. Throughout his life, he worked as a laborer, making products and building structures that helped with the growth of Fairfax and Arlington Counties. In his spare time, he masterfully whittled wood into pieces of art, undoubtedly a skill handed down to him from his African ancestry. Raymond also had excellent handwriting. His cursive writing looked like a form of art.

Another skill certainly handed down to him was the ability to concoct poultices to treat minor cuts and abrasions. Often, as a child, I played outside with my siblings and other children and sometimes sustained cuts and abrasions to my elbows, knees, legs, etc. To treat these injuries, Raymond concocted and applied poultices to them. To my surprise, the injuries healed rapidly. The use of traditional remedies for healing was a basic part of the African tradition, and undoubtedly this practice was also handed down to him from his African ancestry.

DOROTHY BELLE (JACKSON) SMITH (1916–1957)
MOTHER OF CONSTANCE B. SMITH

By Constance B. Smith

Dorothy Belle Jackson Smith. *Photo courtesy of Constance B. Smith.*

Ron Crittendon, son; Connie Smith, mother; and Vickie Lucas, daughter, in front of the family marker at Jermantown Cemetery. *Photo courtesy of Jenee Lindner.*

Dorothy Belle (Jackson) Smith was born in Washington, D.C., on May 21, 1916, and she died in Arlington, Virginia, on May 18, 1957. Her parents were Raymond Lewis Jackson and Hattie Kye Jackson. Her siblings were Thelma Mae, Ethel Elizabeth, William Lewis, Ernest Eugene and Harold Kye. She is buried in the Jermantown Cemetery in Fairfax, Virginia, with all her siblings except for Thelma Mae, who was buried in the Pleasant Valley Cemetery in Annandale, Virginia.

Dorothy was married to Leonard Wardworth Smith Sr. on March 28, 1943, in Arlington, Virginia, and they had three children: Paul Kenneth Smith, Constance Bernita Smith and Leonard Wardworth Smith Jr. Dorothy also had a daughter named Myrtle Lee Jackson Spencer.

Dorothy was a homemaker. She was known as a great dancer. She and her dance partner, her cousin Eddie, competed in local amateur dance contests. They danced the Lindy Hop. The Lindy Hop was an American swing dance that was born in the African American communities in Harlem, New York, in 1928. It was a very popular dance during the late 1930s and early 1940s.

I surmise that my great grandfather named Lewis E. Jackson was born in Providence, Fairfax, Virginia. He died on December 22, 1929, and was buried in Jermantown Cemetery because (1) he was a member of the Mt. Calvary Baptist Church (clerk) and (2) he was a member of the Colored Lodge #4 Burial Sons and Daughters of the Benevolence of Fairfax

County. His name has been added to the Jermantown Cemetery grave list. Malvina Jackson, his wife, has her headstone and is on the list. My great-great grandparents named Henry Jackson and Lucy/Lucie Richards Jackson are probably buried in the cemetery. My great-great-great grandparents named Lewis Jackson and Celenia Jackson are also probably buried in the Jermantown Cemetery.

JOHN COLLINS (1615–1693)
TWELVE-TIMES-GREAT-GRANDFATHER

By Jenee Lindner

I came across an out-of-print book called *Shades of Gray: A Beginning—The Origins and Development of a Black Family in Fairfax, Virginia*, written by Hareem Badil-Abish. His cousin Dennis Howard put it together in book form at the bidding of his dying relative, after organizing his research. It goes on for well over two hundred pages.[92]

Jenee Lindner at the segregated Sons and Daughters of Liberty Cemetery at the Pines, Annandale, Virginia. It is in Fairfax County, a few miles from Jermantown Cemetery. *Photo courtesy of Jenee Lindner.*

As I read, I came across the Collins family, which intermarried with the Gibbons, Parkers, Paynes, Colberts and many other local Black families. Hareem was able to go back to a European relative who came to Jamestown, Virginia, in 1635 named John Collins. When I saw this name, I burst into tears. Why? I looked at my own genealogy to double check. Yes, I am directly related to him, too. Our families lived together for about ten generations. His family line moved north around the 1800s and eventually settled in Fairfax County.

My Collins family line went down to North Carolina in the 1800s. Eventually, my second-great grandparents, Albert Washington Collins (1814–1873) and his wife, Susan Newman Thomas Collins (1818–1849), moved and homesteaded in Mississippi. They joined the Church of Jesus Christ of Latter-day Saints there in the 1840s, freed their enslaved and moved West. They went with several in the community across the plains and settled in Utah and, later, California.[93]

No wonder I was so drawn to this work. Can the lament of my heart be answered in such a wondrous way? I have more genealogy to do for my family who were lost to me but now are found. My healing process has come full circle. We are family. A special thank-you from me to our esteemed ancestors for impressing on my mind to know your names.

Chapter 4

TIMELINE OF JERMANTOWN CEMETERY

by Jenee Lindner

1838: The national organization of the Colored Benevolence Society is founded.

1868: William Rumsey and his wife sell land (about one acre) to the trustees of the Colored Burial Sons and Daughters for the Benevolence of Fairfax Court House Virginia.[94] Trustees: Alfred Whaley, Thomas Sinkfield, Milton Brooks.

November 17, 1887: Request is made for change of trustees for negligence, which included seventeen signatures supporting the change.[95] Retired trustees: Jack Rowe, Alfred Whaley, Thomas Sinkfield. New trustees appointed: Horace Gibson, Strother Gibson, James Henderson.

1923: All Colored Benevolence Society chapters are dissolved, including the Fairfax Courthouse chapter.

January 1930: Trustees to replace the former organization called the Fairfax Colored Cemetery Association include Walter Bowles, George Hunter, James Hunter, Ellen Gray, Antonia Payne.[96]

1989: A *Connection* newspaper article discusses Reverend Booker Taylor's attempt to have Jermantown Cemetery listed in the National

School Street area children while a parent takes a picture before letting them go in their house dressed in their Sunday best. *Standing*: Michael Colbert and Cheryl Colbert; *seated*: Mark Colbert and Tonya Metcalf. *Photo courtesy of Rita Colbert.*

Register of Historic Places. Reverend Taylor collected 137 signatures in favor from his congregation, the members of Mount Calvary Baptist Church in Fairfax, Virginia. The cemetery is not listed today, nor was it ever listed. We speculate that the city did not give its support to move forward.

October 17, 2014: Jermantown Cemetery Trusteeship is created, with Dennis Howard as founder and president on behalf of the Jermantown Cemetery Grave Preservation Association nonprofit.

February 28, 2015: Jermantown Cemetery Grave Preservation Association, nonprofit, is officially registered by the Fairfax County Circuit Court with Dennis Howard as founder and president.

2019: Jermantown Cemetery Grave Preservation Association nonprofit expires.

2020: Local grassroots Christian community racial justice and healing programs called racial reconciliation groups (RRGs) commemorate those buried at the Jermantown Cemetery with homemade wreaths by Jeanne Ayivorh, Tony Zipfel, Inece Bryant, Carl Reid, Debbie Lynch, Buz Schmidt, Will Rowe, Robert MacKay, Eric and Karen Newton, Kit Hogye, Ella Lattimore, Mary Jo Copeland, Tom Pritchard, Felix Wilson, David Smith, David White, Kristyne Torruella, Maynard Henry, Wendy Hart, Jenee Lindner, Peggy Tadj, Robert MacKay and many others for Christmas and Juneteenth.

July 2021: Jenee Lindner, history commissioner and local RRG representative, facilitates the creation of a new Jermantown Cemetery organization. The group starts in her home, and by permission of Reverend Jeffery Johnson, meetings continue at Mount Calvary Baptist Church in Fairfax, Virginia.

October 4, 2021: Jermantown Cemetery Preservation Society, nonprofit, is created, with Ron Crittendon as president, Linneall Naylor as vice president and Constance B. Smith as secretary/treasurer.

November 2021: Will Rowe, Carl Reid and other Booz Allen Hamilton Inc. volunteers take individual pictures of gravestones with GPS and of any ground depressions they can see or were told about by cemetery descendants at each gravesite. Tony Zipfel and Carl Rowe record descendants and others on-site.

Spring–Summer 2022: Dr. Jason Boroughs, research archaeologist at George Washington's Mount Vernon, with George Washington University students, undertakes a ground penetration radar survey; 138 grave depressions are found.

August 28, 2022: First Jermantown Cemetery Legacy Day by Jermantown Cemetery Preservation Society for all descendants is held. An RRG arranges to have it at the Truro Anglican Church in Fairfax. RRG helps logistically, plus cooking and donating food served.

Fall 2022: Jermantown Cemetery Preservation Society nonprofit leadership now consists of Linneall Naylor as president, Rondia Prescott as vice president; Vicki Lucas as sergeant at arms and Constance B. Smith as secretary/treasurer.

June 23, 2023: Jermantown Cemetery Trusteeship is approved by Fairfax County Circuit Court judge Grace Burke Carroll, with new trustees Dayna Burns, Linneall Naylor, Vickie Lucas, Rita Colbert and Rondia Prescott, all cemetery descendants.

August 19, 2023: Second Jermantown Cemetery Legacy Day by Jermantown Cemetery Preservation Society for all descendants is held at historically Black Mount Calvary Baptist Church, Fairfax.

PART II.

SEGREGATED COMMUNITIES IN FAIRFAX, VIRGINIA

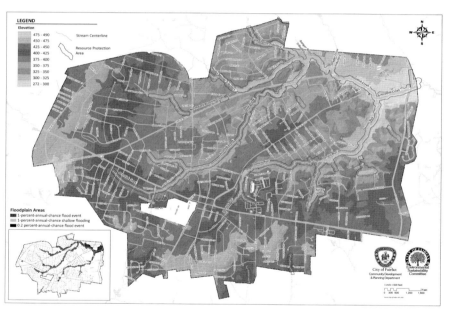

Fairfax City map with creeks. When herders (a person who looks after a herd of livestock or makes a living from keeping livestock, especially in open country) and drovers (one who drives cattle or sheep) were moving animals from sometimes as far away as beyond the Shenandoah Mountains to Washington, D.C., the Little River Turnpike was a good, viable option. After such a long walk, they needed to clean the animals before taking them to the farmer's market in Washington, D.C., to be sold. Fairfax was about a day's walk of sixteen miles from Washington, D.C. With water around in abundance, Fairfax was full of creeks and streams to drive them across and wash off some of the dirt from their long journey. *Streams, Resource Protection Area, and Elevation of the City of Fairfax, Virginia, https://www.fairfaxva. gov/services/about-us/city-maps.*

Chapter 1

BEFORE 1868: LIFE, LABOR AND
THE LITTLE RIVER TURNPIKE

By Jenee Lindner

Richard Ratcliffe bought three thousand acres of land scattered about in the greater Fairfax area to sell or rent.[97] He became the driving force for the new county seat named Providence (created in 1805).[98] Ratcliffe moved from Alexandra, Virginia, with his wife and nine children around 1787. He kept for himself a large six-hundred-acre property called Mount Vineyard Plantation. Ratcliffe built a mansion and family grave site next to the house, completed by 1790.[99] It was west of the Fairfax Courthouse. It would be built along Main Street with the cross street of Oak Street today.[100] Ratcliffe brought thirty-five servants and enslaved with him.[101]

According to historian Ed Trexler, these laborers and their families, except the house servants, lived half a mile away, closer to the present Jermantown Cemetery land where Route 50 (old Little River Turnpike) is today. The present Jermantown Cemetery was the northwest corner of Ratcliffe's property.[102] Trexler believes it was a graveyard before being named Jermantown Cemetery in 1868. Trexler wrote:

The custom at that time when most people lived on a family farm was that the dead were buried in family plots somewhere near the house in which they lived. Generally, if possible, the burial plot would have been to the east of the house. The enslaved, and other members of the "extended family," would likewise be buried near their [enslaved] quarters, and most often, to the east of these quarters. These dwellings were generally located in a safe spot close to the work area and usually away from the main house.

The Ratcliffe family cemetery can be found today to the east of where the Ratcliffe family manor house once stood. The burial spot of Jermantown Cemetery is located to the east of where it is believed the Ratcliffe family [enslaved] quarters once stood; both meeting the customs of the time.[103]

Enslaved graveyards were also different than other cemeteries. The use of *graveyard* rather than *cemetery* is deliberate here. *Cemetery* suggests more care, perhaps an area more structured in design. I also believe this ancestral plot of land became a graveyard first and a cemetery second. Those buried there are no longer forgotten—perhaps unmarked, but certainly not unsung.[104]

There is a small stream called Accotink Creek that borders the Jermantown Cemetery on the west side. It gave me answers. (I was a little deflated when I recently saw that it now flows underground through a large pipe.) The sound of water can be very soothing to one's soul. As for this Jermantown stream, you could jump over it if you had a running leap. I suspect there were makeshift bridges and boards to make it less hazardous. It divided the land of the living and the dead in two halves, perfectly, as was the custom in Africa. The enslaved lived on the west side, where they toiled and worked, ate and slept, cried and laughed and lived a life with as much dignity as they could. The graveyard was "across the river" on the east side, waiting for their next chapter on the road to eternity.

I read an article called "Down by the Riverside: Burial Practices of the Enslaved" from the Coracle interfaith racial unity group.[105] Sarah Kohrs, the author, talks about how Africans wanted graveyards to be near a water source. The reverence given to water as it sustains life, from Africa to America, is a central symbol in most all religious beliefs. Ancestors are considered bridges between heaven and man.[106] As for the body of the deceased, some tribes washed it with water, others with traditional medicines or oil; some covered the body with cloth, leaves or even leather. Some religious traditions in Africa laid the deceased in water and later buried their bones. The location of burials near water also gave a spiritual dimension to the afterlife. The Edo

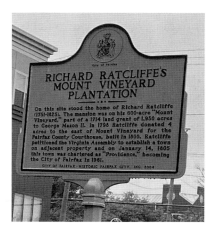

Richard Ratcliffe's Mount Vineyard Plantation marker. *Courtesy of the Historical Marker Database, HMdb.org.*

people in Nigeria believed that the soul embarked in a canoe to cross the sea to the spirit world.[107]

As those brought from Africa embraced Christian theology, their songs began to describe a water baptism, which is a spiritual cleansing that occurs when someone is initiated into Christianity. A woman named Sarah Fitzpatrick said, "Back in the old days we did not have embalmers. When a person died, we had to hurry and put them in the ground. Then, later we had a big funeral. We had big dinners and preaching."[108]

Around 1800, there were about forty enslaved of all ages living in the Jermantown area on Richard Ratcliffe's plantation.[109]

Fairfax Court House

As a county sheriff and sitting judge, Ratcliffe sold four acres for one dollar to build a new county seat. In June 1799, Ratcliffe transferred the land to Fairfax County, which accepted his offer of four acres of land for a new courthouse, jail and related offices. The courthouse was completed in 1800.[110] Soon, Sheriff Ratcliffe deeded more land to the courthouse lot because it was too small to accommodate a clerk's office, jail, pillory, stocks, stable and all the other buildings that would be required. Accordingly, in March 1800, the court ordered the acquisition of an additional six acres. No record exists of the acquisition of an additional six acres from Richard Radcliffe, but on March 13, 1800, "in obedience to the order of the court," ten acres were laid off to create the town limits.[111] "Providence" was established around the Fairfax County Courthouse in 1805 (nickname: Fairfax Courthouse). The name changed in 1859 to Fairfax. It was incorporated as a town in 1874. It became the City of Fairfax by court order in 1961.[112]

Little River Turnpike

The location of the courthouse soon influenced events to Richard Ratcliffe's benefit. It also gives us an understanding of what those enslaved by him were doing. We have learned that some of them built the first community roads and infrastructure besides farming. Construction of the Little River Turnpike began in 1802 in Alexandria. It was completed nine years later at the Little River in present-day Aldie in 1811.[113] As a byproduct, the turnpike gave access to Ratcliffe's land, thereby increasing the land's value. It was also

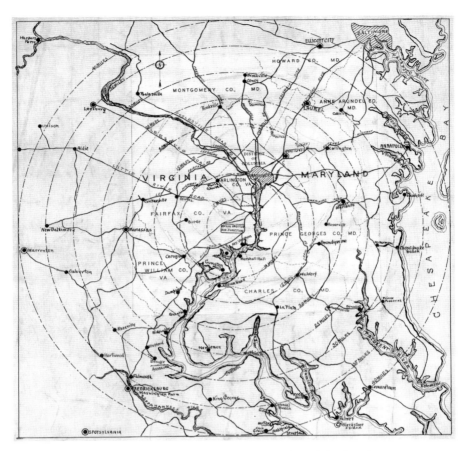

An aerial map of the metropolitan area from the 1920s. One of the first airports was in Fairfax County on Beacon Hill on Route 1. The Wright Brothers won a contract to transport mail to the federal government. This was a very important stop. The entire Little River Turnpike is mapped to follow by air as a sight landmark from Alexandria to the hamlet of Aldie. Aldie was known for its large water-driven mill. At Aldie is a river that is noted on this map but still important for air navigational purposes, too—called Little River, hence the name of the turnpike. *Library of Congress.*

a way for Ratcliffe to enrich himself off the toil and work of the enslaved. As his enslaved developed specialty skills, he could sell their skills in building roads and in road work. He, not the laborer, would be paid most of the income for services rendered. This was a common practice among owners of the enslaved.

The only caveat to this unfair system was that the servant or enslaved person could potentially negotiate their specialty skills to garnish some of their earnings back to themselves. This is how many bought their freedom to became free in a slave society and earned money to free their families.

The turnpike would improve travel for farmers who conveyed their goods from the western counties, and it connected the Shenandoah Mountains by a better-maintained road to the port of Alexandria, Virginia. The road, almost thirty-four miles in length, was constructed using enslaved labor, which involved clearing the proposed route of trees and vegetation, quarrying gravel and crushing stone. It was the first American turnpike here in northern Virginia.[114]

According to Connie Ring (former Fairfax County Circuit Court historian and manager), as detailed in her biography of Richard Ratcliffe: "It is believed that Ratcliffe's slaves may have built a nine-mile section of the road."[115] The new Town of Providence would follow these same fifty-foot-wide street dimensions.[116] These same laborers would build those roads.

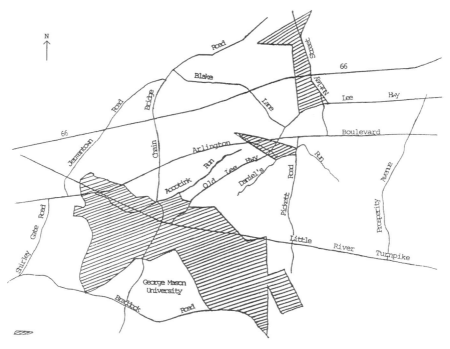

Richard Ratcliffe's Estate Plantation of three thousand scattered acres (*shaded area*). The Fairfax city center is at the crossroads of Little River Turnpike and Chain Bridge Road. *Hand-drawn map courtesy of Constance K. Ring, from her article in* Historical Society at Fairfax County, Virginia, *vol. 25, called "Richard Ratcliffe: The Man, His Courthouse, and His Town," p. 98.*

But according to historian Debbie Robison, these enslaved workers built beyond the nine miles—even more of the thirty-four-mile-long road. She wrote:

> Before there were turnpike roads, local citizens were required to keep roads in good condition. The court assigned sections of roads to men who lived along the route, and if you didn't maintain your section, you could be fined by the court.[117] The Little River Turnpike Company charter called for a 50-feet wide road with a 20-feet wide paved section. The center paved [made of various sizes of gravel hard pressed] section was to be used in wet and winter conditions, the outside unpaved lanes otherwise. The sides were ditched, and stone conduits installed to drain water from the roadway.[118]

Robison wrote further,

> As [Little River Turnpike] construction continued into less populated areas the company experienced labor shortages. Already excluded were landholder men below the age of 16, millers, ferry keepers, ironworks owners and major slave holders. Residents living more than three miles from the construction site could not be called on for statute labor as required by the charter. Consequently, it needed contracted enslaved labor.[119]

There is no indication that the enslaved helped build the first four miles near Alexandria, but for the next section, there is no question that they did, starting in December 1803. The company's contractor, Richard Ratcliffe, wished to hire for the upcoming year twenty "Able bodied Negro Men," making the promise that "good usage to, and punctual payment for their services may be relied on." Ratcliffe continued to use enslaved labor to construct the turnpike in 1808, when he placed another advertisement for "twenty able bodied Negro Men."[120] Many of these men, we surmise, were from the Ratcliffe Plantation and the neighboring Fitzhugh Plantation.

Things did not always go smoothly. In 1804, Ratcliffe posted a ten-dollar reward for Gabriel, an enslaved young man about twenty-one years old, who escaped from bondage while working on the turnpike. In 1805, Jacob, a fifty-year-old enslaved man who was working on the road, fled from the turnpike. A ten-dollar reward for his return was posted by the Little River Turnpike Company. We do not know the outcome.

Toll Gates

Initially, there were seven toll gates, which were opened on the following dates:

Gate 1: October 11, 1806
Gate 2: October 11, 1806
Gate 3: February 1, 1809
Gate 4: February 1, 1809
Gate 5: January 15, 1810
Gate 6: 1812
Gate 7: 1812[121]

Seven gates were built that a group of travelers had to pass by paying a fee for the continuing upkeep of the road. The fourth gate was close to the Little River Turnpike bridge over Difficult Run creek near Jermantown.[122] It was called Shirley Gate. There is a road named after it called Shirley Gate Road.

The new road enhanced the value of property it passed through—an idea promoted in company statements. This was especially true for Richard Ratcliffe. He successfully promoted establishing the town center on his land, in which the new turnpike became its main street.[123]

Difficult Run Bridge in Chantilly, just above Jermantown on the Little River Turnpike. Rondia Prescott and Rita Colbert have records of ancestors repairing the turnpike road. Per the *Fairfax Herald*, Jacob Colbert earned money from the county for labor on the road. *From* This Was Virginia 1900–1927 as Shown by Glass Negatives of J. Harry Shannon, the Rambler, *compiled by Connie and Mayo Stuntz. Courtesy of the Virginia Room, Fairfax County Public Library.*

RICHARD RATCLIFFE'S WILL

Ratcliffe's last census record before his death was in 1820. It gives a breakdown of his household. Richard Ratcliffe would die in 1825.[124]

1820 United States Federal Census
Name: Richard Ratcliffe
Home in 1820 (City, County, State): Truro Parish, Fairfax, Virginia
Enumeration Date: August 7, 1820
Free White Persons—Males—10 thru 15: 1
Free White Persons—Males—45 and over: 2
Free White Persons—Females—10 thru 15: 1
Free White Persons—Females—16 thru 25: 1
Free White Persons—Females—45 and over: 1
Slaves—Males—Under 14: 3
Slaves—Males—14 thru 25: 4
Slaves—Males—26 thru 44: 1
Slaves—Males—45 and over: 3
Slaves—Females—Under 14: 7
Slaves—Females—14 thru 25: 1
Slaves—Females—26 thru 44: 1
Slaves—Females—45 and over: 3
Number of Persons—Engaged in Agriculture: 11
Free White Persons—Under 16: 2
Free White Persons—Over 25: 3
Total Free White Persons: 6
Total Slaves: 23
Total All Persons—White, Slaves, Colored, Other Household Member: 29[125]

Richard Ratcliffe also bequeathed his wealth in his last will and testament written in 1815, ten years before his death in 1825, which gives us clues to the names of those he enslaved:

To my son Charles I give and bequeath my slaves Old George, his wife Sisha, their son Henson and their two youngest Children…I give & bequeath to my daughter Patsey Ratcliffe four young negroes, and to Locian her sister, four young negroes.…My wife to dispose of as she pleases any negroes not already disposed of after my wife's death are to be equally divided among all my children.[126]

A 1960s map of the School Street area where the old horse racetrack was located, showing schools and George Mason University. *Courtesy of Historic Fairfax City, Inc.; map designed by William Page Johnson II.*

We have another important document as we continue to look for those who were forced to work for Ratcliffe. Ratcliffe's estate was inventoried and appraised in June 1826 by the judge-appointed George Mason VI (1786–1834). From his grandson Samuel Farr II: "He presented his assessment to officials in the Fairfax courthouse that of his grandfather, Richard Ratcliffe."[127]

This final probated document priced female "[s]laves," among them Tamar and her daughters Mary, Sarah and Maria. Their resale was estimated at $500. Another woman, Eliza, was appraised at $300, while "Old George" was estimated to be worth $30. When Ratcliffe "departed life" in 1825, he left behind $4,445 in credited assets, ranging from his plantation to agricultural implements and deeds to drinking taverns. The total value of his "Negroes" amounted to $3,519 (equivalent to $100,000 in 2021), roughly 80 percent of the estate's value. Fields, ploughs and pubs aside, enslaved women comprised Ratcliffe's most prized investment.[128]

ENSLAVED IN RICHARD RATCLIFFE'S WILL

An inventory and appraisement of the personal estate of Richard Ratcliffe deceased to apriz [apprise]:	
Negroes, David $1, Ally $1.00, George $1	3.00
Jane West $1, Old George $30, Sasha $30	61.00
Tamar and child Mary $250, Sarah $250, Maria [daughter]	500.00
Eliza $300, John $300, Dennis $325	925.00
Menta $300, John West $ (sold for $600)	300.00

Nace $250, Liddy and Child Henry $150, Peter $250	650.00
Milly her child William $325, Hampton $250	575.00
Dary $250, Hannah $180, Haley a girl $125	505.00
	$3,519.00

Fairfax Will Book, P-0, p. 57, March 29, 1815. *Courtesy of Fairfax Circuit Court Historic Records Center.*

AFTER THE RATCLIFFE FAMILY

Several of Ratcliffe's descendants owned the Mount Vineyard Plantation with these enslaved until 1842, when it was sold out of the family. William Rumsey from New York brought the old farm in 1842.[129] He and his wife became founding members of the Truro Episcopal Church in Fairfax City.[130] The same year the Rumseys moved there, Reverend Richard Templeton Brown, rector of the Episcopal Falls Church, began to hold services in the Fairfax Court House area.

Initially, services were held in the actual courthouse. However, the use of public property was protested by other churches. Subsequently, Caroline Rumsey agreed to have the service held in their home, at the Mount Vineyard mansion.[131] William Rumsey later set aside a half-acre lot in the southeast corner of his property for the church when selling fifteen acres to Dr. Frederick Baker for a future school for young ladies called Coombs Cottage or the Fairfax Ladies Seminary.[132] The church was built next door around 1845.[133] Rumsey sold the area adjacent to the Truro Episcopal (now Anglican) Church to Reverend Richard Brown, who built a rectory where he lived on a hillside above the church.

Rumsey operated Mount Vineyard as a plantation for several years before he began selling off larger lots. Mount Vineyard had been reduced to about four hundred acres before the Civil War, including another 103-acre tract that Rumsey sold to Sammy Brown of New York in 1856.[134] It was returned to Rumsey for lack of payment after the Civil War in 1867.[135] A part of this disputed area includes where the Jermantown Cemetery site is located today. The concrete wall now found along the back edge of the shopping center was the border of the Brown tract.[136]

The Civil War occurred from 1861 to 1865. At that time, the village of Jermantown was small. Most of the homes in Jermantown were burned by Civil War troops on the Union side on their way to the First Battle of Bull Run, or the Battle of First Manassas, in July 1861.[137]

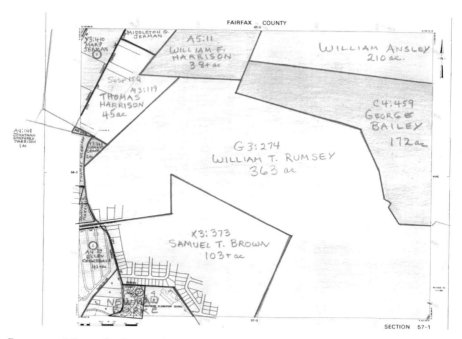

Rumsey and Brown land grants in 1860. Brown would default during the Civil War. The land would be returned to Mr. and Mrs. Rumsey. They would sell one acre for the segregated Jermantown Cemetery. 1860 Tax Map 57-1. *Courtesy of Fairfax Circuit Court Historic Records Center.*

The Battle of Chantilly/Ox Hill, which took place on September 1, 1862, was the largest Civil War battle in Fairfax County.[138] There would be 1,500 casualties. This battle included the area where the Fair Lakes Mall is today and radiated out to West Ox Road and Monument Drive in Fairfax, Virginia. It included thousands of soldiers around Jermantown. Historian Ed Trexler wrote,

> *In the late 1990s, records were found in the National Archives documenting the 1865 removal of the bodies of 35 unnamed Union soldiers from the Mount Vineyard Estate. This record was among the records of the 1500 soldiers who died and were removed after the battle. There is a special written note which states: "removed from Mount Vineyard Cemetery November 23, 1865." All this information was about 100 pages long on old, yellowed paper.*[139]

Clergy from a soldier's home unit would return to dig up the bodies and send them home or to be buried in a military cemetery. Jermantown Cemetery is the closest cemetery plot to the battlefield if previously used as a burial ground. It would have made sense to bury soldiers there just off Little River Turnpike as opposed to the Ratcliffe mansion's family graveyard, a mile farther at the intersection of Main Street and Oak Street.[140]

Reverend Brown fled Fairfax during the Civil War, and during that time, his hilltop rectory was demolished by troops. It has been documented that Union soldiers sought bricks to make temporary chimneys for their winter huts in 1862. We know nearby Payne's Church, on Ox Road, was demolished in this manner, brick by brick.[141] It could have happened to Reverend Brown's rectory, too. On December 31, 1866, one year after the Civil War ended, the trustees of the Ladies Memorial Association paid Reverend Richard T. Brown and his wife, Marion, $225 for 2⅓ acres. This hillside plot would become the Fairfax Memorial Cemetery.[142] At first, African Americans could not be buried there (they can now).

After 1865, some African Americans from Mount Vineyard continued to live in the Jermantown area after being freed, having established homes while on the old Ratcliffe farm near the cemetery. For example, Alfred Whaley's

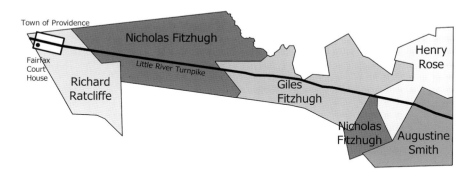

Locally, the Little River Turnpike was built through the land of Richard Ratcliffe, Nicholas Fitzhugh, Giles Fitzhugh, Nicholas Fitzhugh, Henry Rose and Augustine Smith. We suppose that many of their enslaved from this area worked on building the road. It is interesting to note that Black women were needed during this time to wash clothes and perform other domestic tasks. The children came along to be supervised. It could be a family job if their enslavers were so inclined. It was not all the time, but we do have evidence through pictures near Alexandria of a Black woman washing clothes with young children surrounding her as a part of a later road repair crew. *Map created by Sam Lindner, based on a map on Braddock's Gold website.*

family descendants lived only two doors down from the cemetery into the twentieth century. They sold food and blacksmithing services to drovers, who were movers of livestock—usually sheep, cattle and horses—"on the hoof" over long distances and herders who managed, bred or tended to livestock—including pigs, chickens and geese—and transported animal feed, using wagons or carts, traveling the turnpike.[143] Others that were already free before the Civil War had done the same.

FITZHUGH FAMILY AND THE RAVENSWORTH PLANTATION

The large estate south of Richard Ratcliffe's was called the Ravensworth Estate. A total of over two hundred enslaved worked there. They may have worked on the Little River Turnpike, as well. Owned by the Fitzhugh family, the turnpike crossed lands owned by them, including relatives or friends Nicholas Fitzhugh, Giles Fitzhugh, Henry Rose and Augustine Smith.

In a January 1850 Fairfax County court session, the first of sixty-one formerly enslaved African Americans registered as free Blacks, who were manumitted under the provisions of William Henry Fitzhugh's will. It had been twenty years since William Henry (1792–1830) died, while his will stated, "After the year 1850, I leave all my negros unconditionally free."[144]

RAVENSWORTH PLANTATION ENSLAVED MANUMITTED IN 1850 BY WILLIAM FITZHUGH

NAME	AGE
Thomas Anderson	35
Rob Anderson	21
Sarah Ann Bennett	22
Charles Brown	45
Betty Brown	40
William Burke	65
Melinda Burke	58
James Burke	55
Sanford Gutler	26

NAME	AGE
Abraham Gwin	65
Alfred Gwin	35
Violet Burke	53
John Burke	51
Hilliard Burke	34
Wesley Burke	30
Albert Burke	29
Leah Burke	29
Dulany Burke	27
Lorenzo Burke	25
Washington Burrells	37
William Butcher	62
James Butcher	40
Louisa Butcher	40
Lilly Butcher	25
Ann Butcher	21
Going Butler	65
Grace Cambridge	45
Robert Clark	45
Betsey Dade	26
Sally Dixon	25
Bryan Douglas	30
Jesse Douglas	30
Emanuel Douglas	28
Shirley Douglas	28
Henry Douglas	26
Melinda Douglas	25
Stuart Douglas	23
Henry Geeson	33
Mary Geeson	30

NAME	AGE
Laura Gwin	28
William Huff	28
John Jeffries	50
Carter Lee	35
Harry Parker	58
Kitty Parker	56
John Parker	27
George Parker	22
John Rhodes	30
Henry Ross	55
Cynthia Ross	53
Henry Ross	30
Caroline Smith	36
Armistead Triplett	27
Virgil Ward	64
Lelia Ward	37
Henry Ward	36
Cato Ward	27
Virgil Ward	23
George Ward	21
Sally Williams	30
Lucinda (none given)	27

Fitzhugh plantation enslaved manumitted twenty years after the death of William Henry Fitzhugh (1792–1830). His will stated: "After the year 1850, I leave all my negros unconditionally free." *Courtesy of Fairfax Circuit Court Historic Records Center.*

Chapter 2

JERMANTOWN COMMUNITY HISTORY

By Etta Willson, Rita Colbert, Linneall Naylor, Rondia Prescott and Jenee Lindner

Many Fairfax City, Virginia African Americans lived in the Jermantown area before and after the Civil War due to enslaved living quarters likely being located there on Richard Ratcliffe's Mount Vineyard Plantation.[145] Freed African Americans were attracted to the area by the commerce-rich Little River Turnpike.[146]

Page Johnson, a well-known local historian, wrote:

> *In 1862, the village of Jermantown was an unincorporated place named for the family of Hezekiah and Mary Ann (Robey) Jerman. The Jerman farm occupied 96 acres and stood on northwest corner of the intersection of the Little River Turnpike (Rt. 236/Main St.) and the Flint Hill Road (Jermantown Road)* [near the Route 66 interchange].[147]

During the Civil War, Jermantown was described as a collection of eight to ten houses, a principal store (over which flew alternately a flag of secession and the stars and stripes), a telegraph office and a blacksmith's shop. The village also had "a good well which delighted the troops, but as a place it is exceedingly contemptible…a mean group of buildings which the North would not dignify into a village."[148]

At the time, Jermantown included all the land within the triangle created by Flint Hill Road on the west and the Little River Turnpike on the north, to its intersection with the Warrenton Pike (US 29) on the south.[149]

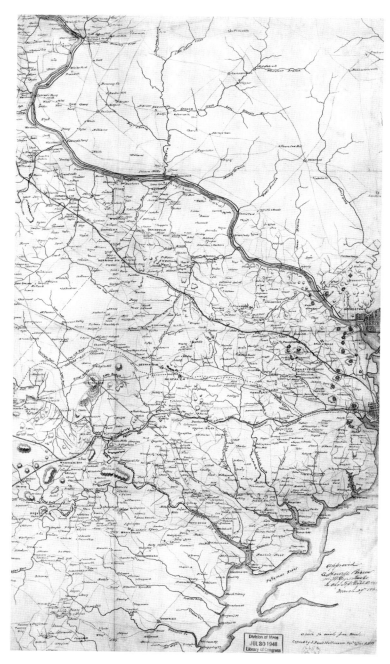

Civil War map of Fairfax area with fortifications, including "Germantown" area. *A map of Fairfax County, and parts of Loudoun and Prince William Counties, Va., and the District of Columbia"; Library of Congress.*

After the Civil War, the Jerman family operated a drovers' rest stop next to their farm.[150] Drovers were those who drove animal herds, either by walking them or in animal carts—in this case, to Washington, D.C. markets from as far away as the Shenandoah Mountains.[151] I have read snippets in early Fairfax newspapers complaining about the animal noises from pigs, geese and dogs running loose in the town at night. Peoples' windows would have been open to the air when it was warm. Of course, the blacksmith and repair shops for horses and oxen-drawn vehicles were there. And let's not forget the cattle on their way to the Washington, D.C. market. What a symphony of sound that must have been, day and night![152]

At the turn of the century, Jermantown was still agrarian, according to resident Vincent D. Sutphin (1917–2014), whose family moved from Fairfax to the Jermantown area in 1924[153] and who wrote about his life and many of those who resided there. The book is called *Nothing Remains the Same: Jermantown, Legato, Pender, and Waples Mill during the 1920s and 1930s in Fairfax County, Virginia*. He worked on the Jerman family's ninety-acre farm with the house located near the intersection between Waples Mill Road, Jermantown Road and the Route 66 freeway on-ramp.[154]

Sutphin stated,

> *Later, a new owner, Mr. Haynes farmed there* [old Jerman family farm] *and was in the huckster business selling chicken eggs and other produce to the Washington market. Some of the first money I earned was paid to me by his son, Russell Haynes, who ran it from 1919 to about 1960. I thinned corn for him as I grew older. He also employed me to help with the huckster business and the sale of products at the old Washington farmers market at 5th and K St NW and the 5th St and Florida Ave NE. This was a great experience and continued during my high school years.*[155]

This was something many did.

Old-timer Vincent Sutphin listed the African American families he remembered in the Jermantown area in the 1920s and 1930s. He marked where they lived on a hand-drawn map copied into his book. Here are the people he knew, with a new map overlay of our streets today: Lucy Jackson; Cindy Lucas; John Jackson (Lucy's husband; worked for George Beach); Becky Ashton (worked for S.P. Twombly); Fred Ashton (son of Becky); Winfree Runner; Ben Runner; Buck Horton (lived in Fairfax) ; Nancy Bernaugh; Washington Payne (worked for George Beach) ; Charity Payne (Washington Payne's wife); Charley Payne (son of Washington and Charity

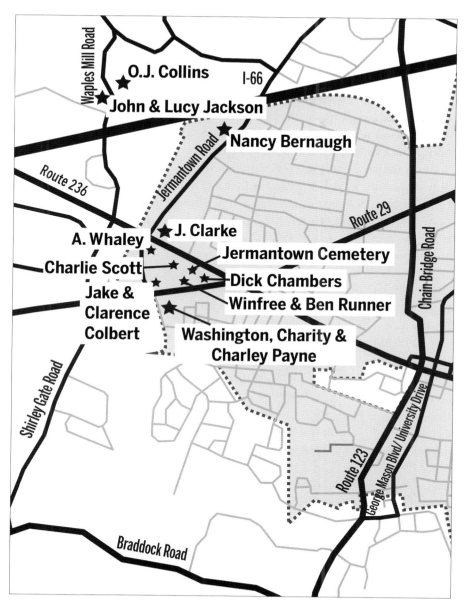

African Americans in Jermantown, Fairfax, Virginia: 1920s–1930s by Vincent Sutphin: *Nothing Remains the Same: Jermantown, Legato, Pender and Waples Mill During the 1920s and 1930s in Fairfax County, Virginia. Map created and typeset by Sam Lindner and Arcadia Publishing.*

Payne); John Colbert; Clarence Colbert (son of Jake Colbert); Charles Scott and his wife; J. Clark and his wife, Margaret (sister of Cindy Lucas); a Mr. Whaley and his wife; Dick Chambers and wife; O.J. Collins; Malinda Payne; and Washington Payne (son of Malinda).[156]

What about the next decade? After more discussions about Sutphin's map, longtime residents Rita Colbert and Etta Willson hand-drew a detailed map of Jermantown to show where their families and friends lived in the 1940s and 1950s. The Jermantown streets were unincorporated and unpaved. You had to go to the post office to pick up your mail.

As Rita said, "Our Jermantown was my world for me as a little girl."[157]

In the 1950s, as car transportation became more affordable for all, visitors to Washington, D.C., could stay in thirty newly built cottages located in a triangular campground area next to the cemetery called Kamp Washington.[158] It included the area where Route 29/Lee Highway and Route 50/Fairfax Boulevard (formerly Little River Turnpike) merged on each side to form a V. The area was sold out of the Colbert family farm.[159] There is a shopping center there now called Hilltop Shopping Center.

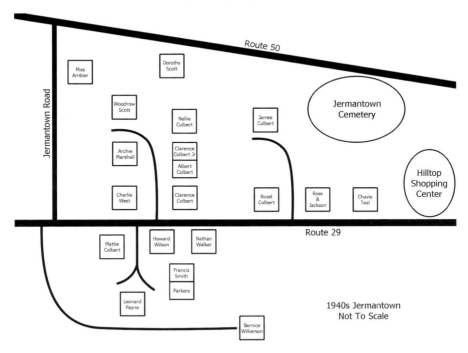

African American Jermantown area, 1940s–1950s. Based on hand-drawn map by Rita Colbert, Etta Willson and Earl Marshall. *Map created and typeset by Sam Lindner, 2022.*

Siblings Dorsie Colbert and Michael Colbert waving in Jermantown, 1950s. *Photo courtesy of Rita Colbert.*

The Jermantown community remained intact until large farms were bought by corporations starting in the late 1950s. Frank Swank and his two sons, John and Ashley, were instrumental in the development of the first commercial property. They owned a large dairy farm. They played a large part in bringing a sewer system to the Route 50 area and I-66 corridor to make it more attractive to buyers. A pumping station was installed on Difficult Run (Creek).[160]

The next year, in 1962, this area was annexed into the city. Fairfax City had been incorporated in 1961. This was its first acquisition to expand the city limits. The acquisition accelerated the changes. It allowed the area to be zoned for commercial development only. Jermantown Road was hard-surfaced, and traffic soon picked up in the area, which meant cattle could not be safe on the road. Eventually, the Route 50-66 Association formed and city plans were adopted, with a master plan to lay pipes for sewers and other public works. Many sold or had to sell per eminent domain in the 1960s, when the area was slowly being developed as shopping centers and other

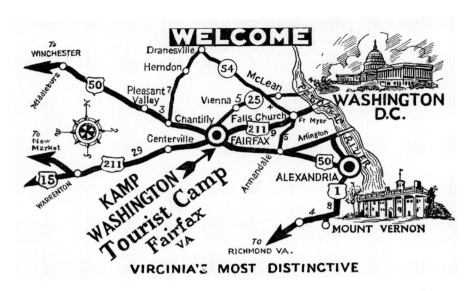

Camp Washington tourist camp just below the Jermantown Cemetery in the 1950s. *Courtesy of the Virginia Room, FCPL.*

commercial venues.[161] African Americans moved to the segregated School Street area or out of the area completely. Rondia Prescott recalls hearing the story of how her grandfather did not want to move. One night, his house mysteriously burned down.

The displaced Jermantown residents' only option in Fairfax City—by this time, where many of them worked—was the School Street area. Other segregated areas close by were in neighboring Vienna, on Zion Drive south of Fairfax, in Ilda east of Fairfax or up by a little satellite community called Hughesville west of Fairfax[162] on Braddock Road. These segregated communities became very close-knit and limited to most outsiders.

Chapter 3

SCHOOL STREET COMMUNITY HISTORY

By Etta Willson, Rita Colbert, Linneall Naylor, Rondia Prescott and Jenee Lindner

This land has a long history of settlement starting in 1800 with the founding of the courthouse and town in 1805. William Page Johnson II wrote an excellent Historic Fairfax City Inc. newsletter article about a horse racetrack that was built here as the town was formed.

This is what he wrote, in part:

> In 1802, Richard Ratcliffe built a course for racing horses at Fairfax Court House. The Fairfax Race Field, also known as the race ground or race course, was located south of the courthouse on the boundary between the present-day City of Fairfax, Fairfax County and George Mason University.
>
> The exact location of the race field was a twenty-five-acre parcel of land bounded by present-day Chain Bridge Road...on the west, School Street on the north, University Drive on the south and just west of Sideburn Road on the east. Present-day George Mason Boulevard, between School Street and University Drive, bisects the site and marks the approximate center of the former race field....
>
> In his will, written in 1815, Richard left the race field to his sons Robert and John....John Ratcliffe died before his father, sometime around 1818 [due to alcoholism and poor habits brought on by "riotous living"]. Subsequently, the race field went to surviving son Robert Ratcliffe....
>
> In the late 18th century and throughout much of the 19th century, horse racing was the main organized sporting event in Virginia and America. The

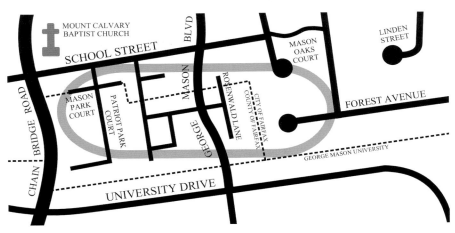

Race field at Fairfax Court House. "The course is handsome equaled by few on the continent and in good order," said John Radcliffe on August 23, 1811. In the late eighteenth century and throughout much of the nineteenth century, horse racing was the main organized sporting event in Virginia and the United States. The sport attracted thousands. It was not unusual for competitors and spectators alike to travel great distances to attend these significant social events. Nearly all jockeys in Virginia were African Americans enslaved by horse owners. *Map created by Sam Lindner after a map by William Page Johnson II.*

sport attracted thousands. It was not unusual for competitors and spectators alike to travel great distances to attend these significant social events. By the late 18th century nearly every inhabited place in Virginia had its own race field....

Races were held several times each year. Spring races and fall races were typical. Race organizers offered purses to winning horses from entrance fees charged to competitors, spectators and vendors. At Fairfax Court House and elsewhere the purse was hung from the starting pole on the day of the race.

The entrance fees charged weren't always necessarily money. In 1829, the fee for entering a race at Louisa, Virginia, was "100 bushels of merchantable wheat." Organizers also charge vendors fees to operate booths, or concession stands, where liquor, food, and other items were sold. Aside from the purse, the main attraction for winning competitors was lucrative stud fees an owner could charge following the race if his horse won. There was also the prestige associated with having a winning horse.

For spectators, the main attraction of horse racing was gambling, with the conception of alcohol being a close second.... Typical wagers included money, tobacco, slaves, and property. Races were generally started by firing a pistol, sounding a trumpet, or hitting a drum. Race organizers employed "proper persons as judges of the Field and Race to settle all disputes that may arise."…

In the late 18th to mid-19th century nearly all jockeys in Virginia were African American slaves. For the owner, the use of slaves was both a cost effective and profitable approach. After all, slaves were unpaid and had intimate knowledge of the temperament and ability of the horses under their care. Slave jockeys were under intense pressure from their owners to win. Their life and work was extremely arduous as most served as rider, trainer, and groom, simultaneously. Typically, they started each day by exercising the horses in their care before breakfast. Slave jockeys also endured physical and mental tortures in exercising their own bodies and restricting food intake to keep their weight down. It wasn't until after the Civil War that the contribution and the role of the jockey began to be accepted. All black jockeys prior to that time remain virtually unknown….

In 1839, Robert Ratcliffe sold the old Fairfax Race Field to his daughter, Jane, and her husband Elcon Jones.[163]

The property was eventually sold out of the family, with Fairfax attorney John S. Barbour purchasing the site for farming in 1909.

AFTER THE CIVIL WAR, the School Street area became the largest welcoming alcove, near the location of George Mason University today on Route 123 (Chain Bridge/Ox Road).[164] Why this area? The School Street area was the general location of the Union Civil War barracks (blockhouses) on

West School Street at sunset. Photo taken by Rondia Prescott. Her grandfather's white Cadillac is clearly visible, parked on the street on the left. *Photo courtesy of Rondia Prescott.*

Willie Mulkey riding his bike in the School Street neighborhood, 1980s. *Photo courtesy of Rita Colbert.*

the Thomas and Sanger farms that were identified in Freedmen Bureau Records as potential housing for the freedmen and families left homeless after the Civil War ended in 1865.[165] The School Street area was near the courthouse and under the protection of the Freedman's Bureau located on the courthouse site.

OUR NEIGHBORHOOD IN FAIRFAX, VIRGINIA

The School Street community had evolved as an unincorporated community. These maps show what the African American community area looked like in the 1950s according to longtime residents Rita Colbert and Etta Willson. To give perspective, in the map opposite (top), the long street on the left is School Street, where the store is located. You will see School Street in more detail in the next two maps (opposite, bottom, and following page). One is east of Chain Bridge Road and the other is west of Chain Bridge Road. The first location of the Mount Calvary Baptist Church was on the corner of Route 123 and Armstrong Street, across from the Fairfax County Circuit Court Government Center. Many lived in that area in between the old church and Braddock Road.

East School Street and West School Street had contained mostly tract homes in the 1950s. This type of home was very common in the greater Fairfax County area. Rust Properties came in, paved School Street and built homes to code. Rust Properties connected everyone to modern-day conveniences. Their mail was delivered rather than having to go to the post office. The children grew up and the adults grew old in comfort and peace for decades until 1989.

The formerly segregated Court House Market still stands on the corner of School Street and Chain Bridge Road. There are those who would like to save it as a heritage site. The leadership in Fairfax City is listening. No one has been there since the deli left during the COVID-19 pandemic.

The Court House Market was built by the Warren Morarity family, who owned it from 1951 to 1978, next to their home on Chain Bridge Road (then

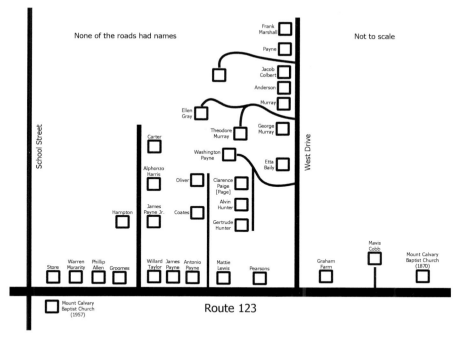

Map of area between School Street and West Street. Based on hand-drawn map by former residents Etta Willson, Rita Colbert and Earl Marshall. *Typeset by Sam Lindner, 2022.*

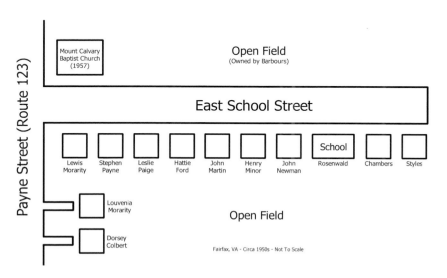

Line map of East School Street based on hand-drawn map by former residents Rita Colbert, Etta Willson and Earl Marshall *Typeset by Sam Lindner, 2022.*

Robinson

Marshall

Thompson   Brooks

Payne   Ford   Jackson   Carter   Harris
Wooded Area

Payne   Metcalf   Clark   Payne
Parking Lot

Warren Morarity (Store Owner)

Courthouse Market

Payne Street (Route 123)

West School Street

Walker   Colbert   Payne   Johnson   Quinn
Cunningham

Wooded Area

Styles   Wright   Smith   Pullen   Allen   Williams   Payne   Colbert

Open Field

Ford

Winston

Fairfax, VA - Circa 1950s - Not To Scale

Line map of West School Street. Based on hand-drawn map by former residents Rita Colbert, Etta Willson and Earl Marshall. *Typeset by Sam Lindner, 2022.*

Court House Market on the corner of School Street and Chain Bridge Road across from the church, 1950s–1980s. *Photo courtesy of the Virginia Room, Fairfax County Public Library.*

Above: Jason Kim and his wife, Sung Kim, were the second owners of the Court House Market, from 1978 to the 2000s. Warren Morarity built it in 1951 and ran it with his nephew Willard Taylor. *Information and photo courtesy of Rita Colbert.*

Left: Paul Taylor, with the Court House Market (*right*) and Morarity family home (*left*) behind him on School Street. Only the market still stands. *Photo courtesy of Rita Colbert.*

Warren Moriarty and Rozel (Jake) Colbert shaking hands. *Photo courtesy of Rita Colbert.*

called Payne Street). There was another store on-site before that one was built, Etta remembers. Etta loved going in to buy a pickle from their giant pickle jar for a nickel, Wise potato chips for a nickel and a miniature bottle of ice-cold Coke for seven cents. From 1958 to 1978, Robert and Dorothy Lockhart rented the market and added the Carryout. They cooked and sold hamburgers and hotdogs in the back. The Carryout was very popular. Dolores

Colbert Dennie was the cook. She was Rita Colbert's aunt, and Rita helped her sometimes. Mike H.: "Dolores helped cook before Jason Kim's wife started doing it." David A.: "That lady could cook."[166] Jason and Sung Kim were the the Court House Market's second owners, from 1978 until the 2000s.

MOUNT CALVARY BAPTIST CHURCH

Two African American churches were erected in this area, furthering

Old Mt. Calvary Baptist Church (May 16, 1870–April 14, 1957) across from Armstrong Street and Chain Bridge Road (near Red Hot and Blue Restaurant today). *Photo courtesy of Lee Hubbard.*

migration. They were the Mount Calvary Baptist Church, founded in May 1870, and the African Methodist Episcopal (AME) Church, founded in December 1870.[167] The AME church would later dissolve and be absorbed into the nonsegregated St. George's United Methodist Church.[168]

The Mount Calvary Baptist Church has continued thriving, having moved a few blocks on Chain Bridge Road to where it is located today. As the present-time Reverend Dr. Jeffery O. Johnson Sr., pastor, states: "Our Biblical Mandate is we are a historical church, founded in 1870 by freed slaves who thought first to build a place of worship before attending to their own needs. Our Biblical mandate comes from the Book of Ephesians. We are here 'For the perfecting of the saints, for the work of ministry, for the edifying of the body of Christ...' EPHESIANS 4:12."[169]

Vision Statement
Mount Calvary will promote the transformation of mankind to conform to the Mandates of God's Word.
The Mission: To disciple the Saints of Mount Calvary by equipping them to impact their families, communities, acquaints, and the World with the Word, Will and Way of God.

Mission Statement
Impacting the Church to Impact the World

Opposite, top: Mount Calvary Baptist Church, 1957–1999. New location on the corner of School Street and Chainbridge Road. *Photo courtesy of Rita Colbert.*

Opposite, bottom: Church building under construction, 1998–99: a newly expanded brick church to replace the white stucco church building in the church parking lot. The white stucco church was demolished afterwards and made into the new church parking lot. *Photo courtesy of Rita Colbert.*

Above: Mount Calvary Baptist Church today. *Photo courtesy of Jenee Lindner.*

Essentials of the Mission
Worship: Adoration and Praise of God
Instruction: Christian Education
Fellowship: Time Invested with the Saints
Evangelism: Time Sharing the Faith with others.[170]

After the Civil War, Christian men and women who settled in and around Fairfax Court House formed an organization for the purpose of soliciting funds to build a church. Some prominent members of this group were Louis Thompson, John Jackson, Strother Gibson, Martin Mellontree and Louis Jackson; there were many others. On May 15, 1870, a parcel of land on Rural Route 123 in the Township of Fairfax near the Fairfax County Courthouse was purchased from landowners Bleeker and Harriet Canfield for the "Colored Baptist Church" with Moses Thompson, Charley Whaley and John Whaley serving as trustees.

Reverend Marshall Downing Williams, DD of Manassas, Virginia, was the first pastor of what would be named Mount Calvary Baptist Church.

135

He was one of the pioneer Missionary Baptist ministers of Northern Virginia and organized and founded this church and many others. The churches together were called the Northern Virginia Baptist Association. During his tenure, Reverend Williams made tremendous contributions in the religious and educational fields. It was noted that his splendid oration and fine Christian bearing marked him as one of the most outstanding ministers of his time. He remained with the church for fifty-four years, until his death on May 17, 1924.

On September 1, 1949, trustees Ernest Pinn, James Hunter, Marvin Metcalf, Atana Payne, Lewis Morarity and John Martin made a down payment to John S. Barbour for a vacant parcel of land at the intersection of Chain Bridge Road and School Street. It was decided to move the church to this new location next to the homes of Deacon James Hunter

Reverend Marshall Downing Williams, moderator of the Northern Virginia Baptist Association and first pastor of Mount Calvary Baptist Church in Fairfax, Virginia. *Photo courtesy of Dayna Burns.*

and Sister Janie Pearson. The cornerstone of the new building was laid in November 1955, with Reverend W.E. Costner, moderator of the Northern Virginia Baptist Association and pastor of Second Baptist Church in Falls Church, Virginia, delivering the sermon. The architect was John Boiling of Falls Church, Virginia, and the builder was Omar Furr of Aldie, Virginia. Design and supervision were by Reverend Milton Sheppard. The last service at the old location was held on April 14, 1957.

Some of the ministers who have served at Mt. Calvary Baptist Church are Reverend Williams, Reverend Lewis, Reverend Richard Botts, Reverend Richard Carter, Reverend Henry Washington, Reverend Winston DeVaughn, Reverend Henry Houston, Reverend Milton Sheppard, Reverend Spencer Coleman, Reverend Clarence Robinson, Reverend Thomas Spears Jr., Reverend Booker W. Taylor, Reverend James G. Austin and, presently, Reverend Dr. Jeffery O. Johnson Sr. The church's current address is 4325 Chain Bridge Road, Fairfax, Virginia 22030.

Here are some clippings from the local newspaper that Reverend Dr. Jeffery O. Johnson Sr. shared:

In front of Mount Calvary Baptist Church, 1940s: Lewis Moriarty, Atana Payne and Marvin Metcalf. *Photo courtesy of Rita Colbert.*

The congregation of Mount Calvary Baptist Church (colored), of which Rev. Marshall Williams is the respected pastor, had a very pleasant and creditable "Children's Day" celebration on Sunday afternoon last.
—Fairfax Herald, *June 19, 1903*

COLORED CITIZENS MEETING. The Fairfax Country-wide colored Citizens Association will hold its regular monthly meeting in Mt. Calvary Baptist Church at Fairfax courthouse. Fairfax, Va. 8 o'clock p.m. Wednesday June 17. Rev. R.W. Brooks, pastor of Lincoln Temple Congregational Church will be the speaker.
—Fairfax Herald, *June 12, 1936*

Colored Citizens. The Fairfax County Colored Citizens Association will hold its regular monthly meeting Wednesday next at 8 p.m., in Mt. Calvary Baptist Church, Fairfax.
—Fairfax Herald, *August 1939*

The Fairfax County Colored Citizens Association will hold its regular meeting in Mt. Calvary Baptist Church, Fairfax, Wednesday next, at 8 p.m. The regular date was changed on account of the blackout. Details of the 1943 crop insurance program will be announced soon after this meeting.
—Fairfax Herald, *19 June 1942*

A fried chicken supper will be served by the Men's Club of Mt. Calvary Baptist Church, Fairfax on March 3 beginning at 5 p.m., at the home of Lewis Morarity. For phone deliveries call Fairfax 473.
—Fairfax Herald, *1951*

The marriage of Miss Alice Virginia Barnes, daughter of Mr. and Mrs. J.H. Barnes, of Fairfax, to Mr. Raymond A. Karshir, of Freeport, 111., took place at 4 o'clock Monday at the Chatham Courts Apartments, Washington. The Rev. James Shera Montgomery, pastor of Calvary Baptist Church, officiated. The bride's only attendant was her sister, Mrs. Ashby Graham, of Fairfax. After the reception, they left for a trip through the West.
—Fairfax Herald, *1952*

MEMORIES OF MOUNT CALVARY BAPTIST CHURCH

Composed by Etta Willson, 2005

I REMEMBER:

A church by the side of the road with old wooden pews; the sun shining brightly through stained glass windows; each window dedicated to the memory of deceased members.

Deaconesses dressed in starched white uniforms and white gloves, hats and shoes; Deacons dressed in black suits and ties.

Little girls in taffeta dresses that swished when they walked; white anklet socks and shiny black patent leather shoes.

Little boys in their Sunday suits; women in hats and gloves and high heeled shoes that matched perfectly.

I REMEMBER:

A wooden floor and a pulpit with red carpet and three ornate chairs; A wood stove that sat in the corner; A choir stand with folding chairs; A black upright piano and an old organ with foot pedals.

A Communion table in front of the pulpit dressed with freshly ironed, white linen cloth; and serving trays with little glasses filled with grape juice and tiny pieces of bread.

Devotional services led by Deacons with bible in hand; keeping the beat with their feet as the church walls seemed to vibrate with the sounds of uplifted voices and fervent prayers.

Powerful testimonies of how God had brought them through dangers seen and unseen; How God had touched their bodies with a finger of love and woke them up and started them on their way.

How the spirit filled the church as the preacher, in his long, black robe, told how you must be born again and salvation was free to all who believed and exhorted sinners to come to Christ.

I REMEMBER:

The choir with rich harmony of high sopranos; strong altos, tenors and resonant bass voices that joyfully filled our hearts with the singing of the old hymns like "Come Thou Fount of Every Blessing," "Jesus Keep Me Near the Cross," and "Amazing Grace How Sweet the Sound That Saved a Wretch Like Me."

As children, we sat near the front of the church as quietly as we could because our parents would give us a "look" if we misbehaved.

Waiting with childish anticipation for the time to go out and play; All the while unaware that we were absorbing what we heard and being shaped and molded by what we experienced.

Hearing the stories of Adam and Eve, Noah, Moses, Joshua and the miracle of Jesus' birth.

Learning that God so loved the world that He gave his only begotten son that whosoever believes in Him should not perish but will have eternal life; that Jesus was crucified and died for our sins and rose on the third day.

I REMEMBER:

Learning at a very young age about God's love, grace, and mercy which has sustained me.

I REMEMBER!

SCHOOLS

All parents were convinced of the importance of education to enable their children to have a better life. While there was some public support for African American schools, they were not funded nearly to the extent of the schools for their White counterparts. A striking example of the separate and unequal conditions of the time can be seen in the very buildings themselves. The Fairfax Elementary School, constructed for Whites in 1873, was a substantial two-story brick building, built on an airy hillside. The building was restored in 1992 and now houses the Fairfax Museum and Visitor Center. By comparison, just down the street, the second African American School, called the Fairfax Colored School, was built about the same time, between 1874 and 1878. It was located at 10565 Main Street east of, and adjoining, the Fairfax City Memorial Cemetery. It was a wooden one-room structure with a single stove for heating in the winter months. It was built in a ravine, along a creek, adjacent to the cemetery. That school was used for approximately fifty years prior to the opening of Rosenwald Elementary School. By 1925, the community had outgrown the old school. A larger school would take its place. The old school lot and building were sold to the Fairfax Cemetery Association in 1927. It was demolished in 1926 because of its dilapidated condition.[171]

Etta Bowles Richards-Strozier (1916–2023), who passed away at age 106, was a student at this school from 1923 to 1925. In 2006, she recalled,

> *The school was built on the side of a hill next to the cemetery. It had one room with a pot-bellied stove in the middle. There was no electricity and no indoor plumbing. The facilities were located outside, and we kids had to get*

1. Mary **Payne** Brooks 2. Virginia **Conic** Payne 3. Sarah **Conic** Payne 4. Mabel **Morarity** Payne 5.Virginia **Payne** Allen 6. Eastern **Payne** 7. Elizabeth **Conic** Primus 8. Edith **Hunter** Collins 9. Lewis **Morarity** 10. Etta **Paige** Bailey 11. Kathleen **Bowles** 12. Herman **Hunter**

Picture was taken on the Fairfax County Fair Grounds in 1916. The students attended the first African American School in Fairfax, then called the "Fairfax Colored School" which was constructed between **1874** and **1878**. It was located on Main Street east of and adjoining the Fairfax Cemetery.

Black school students (grades 1–7) in 1916, before walking in a parade with the banner. The school was located near the Fairfax Memorial Cemetery in a one-room structure with a potbellied stove for heat. *Photo courtesy of Etta Willson and Rita Colbert.*

water from a small spring that flowed in front of the school, or later from a spigot across the street at the Electric Railway Depot.

As a child, Etta walked several miles to school, "through the woods and fields," from her home on Roberts Road. Etta recalled that their teacher, Minnie Beckwith Hughes, Mrs. Hughes came to school in a small horse and buggy. She also remembered,

Because there was no stable, our teacher Mrs. Hughes kept her horse underneath the school. We would occasionally hear him snorting underneath us. One day, because the building was in such bad shape, Mrs. Hughes fell through the rotten floorboards and landed right on that old horse. She wasn't hurt, but it took some time to get her unstuck.[172]

Strozier had fond memories of both the school and of Mr. and Mrs. Hughes. Mrs. Hughes and her husband spent their life in Hughesville.

Their former house still stands. It is located at the intersection of the Fairfax County Parkway and Braddock Road, just outside of the city. Today, the Fairfax County Mott Community Center is next door.

Minnie Beckwith Hughes was the daughter of freed slaves Alfred and Methelda "Fannie" Beckwith. She was born on December 8, 1871, in Fairfax County, Virginia. In 1891, she attended Hampton Institute, now Hampton University, in Hampton, Virginia, and graduated in 1896. As a requirement for graduation, Minnie returned to Fairfax and began student teaching in 1894, at the vacant Hughesville School on Braddock Road. From 1894 to 1903, Minnie taught school at several locations in Fairfax County.[173] Beginning in 1903, she took six years off to give birth to her three children, returning to the classroom in 1909. According to her granddaughter Laurence Nolan, Minnie was teaching school near her home at the time of her marriage.

In the fall of 1916, to make ends meet, Mr. Philipp Edward Hughes, at the age of forty-five and after eighteen years of teaching, went to work for the U.S. Government Printing Office as a full-time skilled laborer. His pay, twenty-five cents per hour, was approximately five times what he had previously earned as a teacher. He held this job until his death on January 10, 1945, at the age of seventy-three.

Minnie Hughes succeeded her husband as the teacher at the Fairfax African American School in 1916. The distance from their home on Braddock Road to the school was approximately three miles, which she traveled by horse and buggy. In the winter months, she usually arrived early enough to light a fire in the central potbellied stove.

The couple lived on a small farm on Braddock Road. The home, which still stands, was located at 12115 Braddock Road just southeast of its intersection with the Fairfax County Parkway. The area was then known as Hughesville. Minnie Beckwith Hughes, teacher at the Fairfax Colored School and first principal of the Fairfax Rosenwald School, died on September 29, 1975, at the age of 103. At the time of her death, she was the oldest pensioner in the history of the Fairfax County Public Schools.[174]

Mrs. Hughes loved her students, and they loved her back, as these notes attest. Mary was determined to make her school a success. During his research, William Page Johnson II found this quote on teaching from Mrs. Hughes:

There is certainly a great deal of talk, but that troubles me very little. There are some things that are very unpleasant here for me, but I am determined to stay here until sent by the proper authorities into another field or dismissed the service entirely....It is not labor for me, as some would call it; I love the work.[175]

The children at the Fairfax Court House Freedmen's School adored their teachers. One teacher, Mary McBride, came down in March 1866 from the Philadelphia Society of Friends and stayed until 1869. Mary had been engaged by the society as a teacher "to locate at any point where a prospect opened [of] being useful."[176] After a vacation, she wrote in a letter to Jacob Ellis:

How pleasant it is to return after absence and find you have been greatly missed, and your appearance hailed with delight. Last Sabbath was reception day with me; at one time I counted fifteen colored visitors, some cried, some laughed, and others looked their happiness—their faces beamed with joy. Some of my children told me yesterday they "knew I would come back." "Why?" "Because we prayed for you night and morning!" I sincerely hope their prayers will not be in vain in other respects. It made me happy to know these poor children had not forgotten. I am quite proud of my pupils. A number of them take particular pride in dressing neatly and nicely, and looking like ladies, two of them especially in the first class. They are good, faithful girls, in whom I have every confidence, and I think in the future they will be able to take entire charge of the school. They are good spellers and readers, write well, and talk grammatically. A number of the young ladies at the boarding school here do not read or write as well as four of the girls in my first class.[177]

In the same letter, McBride also alludes to another pupil, a daughter of the village blacksmith, nine years of age, who kept her father's books and did all his writing, much to the astonishment of the people of Fairfax Court House.

Several children had to walk as many as five miles, each way, to attend the Freedmen's School at Fairfax Court House. Many students attended irregularly. Through necessity, they were hired out by their parents as laborers, especially during the spring planting season and fall harvest. Many students were also without adequate shoes and clothing, even in the winter months. Consequently, illness also caused their absence from school. Early in 1867, Mary McBride reported "two pupils removed by death" and that "attendance has been lessened by sickness."[178]

But in spite of all the hardships, the students were grateful for the opportunity of an education. In spring of 1867, they wrote to their benefactors:

Fairfax Rosenwald School class photo, 1937, including Etta Bowles Strozier (*fourth row, far right*), Mrs. Minnie Hughes (*third row, second from left*); Mrs. Agnes Chaves (*second row, far right*); Warren Hunter (*first row, fourth from right*). *Photo courtesy of Rita Colbert and Etta Willson.*

> *"To the Philadelphia Association of Friends:*
>
> *Ladies and Gentlemen—In the name of the pupils of the colored school of Fairfax C.H. we the undersigned beg leave to thank you for your kindness to us, not only in sending the clothing and gifts, but also in providing us a teacher, books, &c., for a school. We can simply say 'thank you,' and endeavor by our future behavior and improvement to prove that 'actions speak louder than words.'"*
>
> *The above was signed by twenty-one of the pupils, the teacher penciling the ages opposite each name, their ages range from 8 to 16 years—the writer of the address being only thirteen.*[179]

With the start of construction in 1925, on May 7, 1926, Rosenwald Elementary School was dedicated. It was a two-room schoolhouse located at 10515 School Street in Fairfax. Mrs. Hughes was principal. The construction of the Rosenwald Elementary School cost a total of $3,200.[180] The funding for the construction of this school came from three separate places. The first, and the namesake for the school, was the

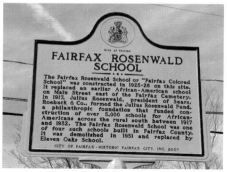

Above: Cousins and still Fairfax Rosenwald school chums today. *Left to right*: Geneva M. Ealy, Simon Atana Payne (named for his uncle) and Etta Allen Willson at the Payne family reunion, August 20, 2022, in Vienna, Virginia. *Photo courtesy of Jenee Lindner.*

Left: Fairfax Rosenwald School Historic Marker on the corner of School Street and George Mason Boulevard. *Photo taken by Jenee Lindner.*

Rosenwald Fund for Education. This organization gave $700 to support the construction of the new school. The Rosenwald Fund was created by philanthropist Julius Rosenwald and Booker T. Washington and helped fund the construction of over five thousand schools for Black children in fifteen southern states. There was a total of four schools funded by the Rosenwald Fund for Education located in Fairfax County. The second source of funds to construct the school was money raised by Black members of the community. The third and final source was money pledged by the Fairfax County School Board in exchange for the Black communities' "continued cooperation."[181]

PROGRAM

ANNUAL FIELD DAY

of all

The Colored Schools

of

Fairfax County, Virginia

at

The New Rosenwald School Building

FAIRFAX, VIRGINIA

Friday, May 13, 1927

Beginning at 10:30 A.M.

Music by a Section of

THE ELKS BAND OF ALEXANDRIA, VA

Under direction of Richard H. Brooks

Above: Rosenwald School with cars on opening day. The school was built with funds from a private donor, the Black community and county school system and was dedicated on May 7, 1926. *Used with permission from Fisk University, John Hope and Aurelia E. Franklin Library, Julius Rosenwald Archives, Special Collections, Nashville, Tennessee.*

Left: Rosenwald School program. *Photo courtesy of Etta Willson.*

Mabel Payne Colbert, interviewed in 2006 at age seventy-seven, was a student at the Rosenwald School beginning in 1935. She recalled,

School was not like it is now. My brothers and sisters and I walked to school from our house on the bottom of School Street. Mrs. Hughes walked to school, too, with her son or grandson. He was crippled and the kids would tease him. She was a kind person.

Our school had a big wood-burning stove, but no indoor plumbing. There was an outhouse out back near the tree line; one side for girls and one side for boys. We did not have a cafeteria, like they do today, until later.

We were very poor and didn't always have the proper clothing. In the winter when it snowed we wore guano sacks around our feet and legs to keep us warm and dry. By the time we got to school, we were half frozen. Mrs. Hughes would pour warm water from a kettle she kept on the stove over our hands to thaw us out. It was hard to learn when you were cold and hungry.

We children also had to help out. We fetched water from the neighbors and had to clean the school before we went home. Everyone had a task.

At recess, we made our own fun. We gathered leaves and played in them, things like that. Sometimes, the older boys would get into trouble and the teacher would have to beat them. Discipline was the rule.[182]

Warren Hunter, interviewed in 2006 at eighty-three, who was a student at the Rosenwald School beginning in 1930, has similar memories,

I went to the Rosenwald School until 7th grade. I lived almost across from City Hall on 123 [Rt. 123], which was part of Mr. Barbour's place at the time. I guess he was one of the richest men in town. My aunt worked for him. My father [James Hunter] worked at Layton Hall Estate, Mr. [Joseph] Willard's farm.

My house was in the black [segregated] part of Fairfax, which included everything south of West Drive. But even though there was segregation, that didn't stop us from playing with the white boys. We would play ball, and other games with them.

We didn't have organized sports activities at school, like they have now. We had "Field Day," which was held annually at the end of the school year. All the black schools would come and compete in races and ball games, that sort of thing. During the school year though, we only had recess. We played a game at recess, which sounds silly now, called "Dogs and Foxes." One group of boys would be the dogs, who would then chase another group of boys who were the foxes. There were lots of woods around the school then to hide in. The game was over when all the foxes had been caught. I enjoyed that game.

We boys also had chores. It was our job to gather the firewood for the fire. You know, there was no such thing as "snow days," like now. It didn't matter if it snowed three feet, Mrs. Hughes, who lived a considerable distance from the school, would always be there and we were expected to be there, too. My, she taught a long time. She taught me, and my brother [Alvin S. Hunter], who went to the old school.

One other thing I remember, when the County finally got a school bus system about '37 or '38, Mrs. Hughes' son, Philip, who we called "Doc," became our bus driver and he drove us to the Jenny Deane School in Manassas, where the blacks went to high school.[183]

Minnie Hughes retired in May 1937. On her retirement her salary was just $65 per month, or $780 per year! She was succeeded as principal by Henrietta B. Brown, 1937–39; America Brown, 1939–40; Lutie L. Coates,

Eleven Oaks Elementary School was a county public school and replaced the Rosenwald School. It was built and opened in May 1953. In 1959, public schools in Virginia began to integrate. Eleven Oaks was closed down in 1966, used for other purposes and then torn down by George Mason University in 2008. *Courtesy of Virginia Room, Fairfax County Public Library.*

1940–44; Bertha L. Waters, 1944–48; Doris R. Jones, 1949–51; and Janie R. Howard, 1951–52.

On September 8, 1953, Eleven Oaks Elementary School opened, with several classrooms and, later, a cafeteria and a playground. It was directly behind Rosenwald Elementary School, and after its completion, Rosenwald was closed and torn down. This new construction cost $223,647 and was significantly bigger than its predecessor.[184] At the time of the school's construction, Jim Crow–era laws dictated that all schools be segregated. Therefore, despite Green Acres Elementary being right around the corner, Eleven Oaks Elementary School was a necessary structure for Black students in Fairfax County.

In 1954, the Supreme Court ruling in the *Brown vs. Board of Education of Topeka, Kansas* case declared segregation in public schools unconstitutional.[185] Virginia's newly installed governor, Thomas B. Stanley, first received the news of the Supreme Court decision calmly and invited both Blacks and Whites to share their views on solving problems created by the court decision. But within the week, Stanley invited Black leaders to his office to urge them to continue to observe segregation and ignore the ruling. This was unacceptable to the Black leaders.[186] Stanley then said publicly, "I shall use every legal means at my command to continue segregated schools in Virginia."[187]

The governor appointed a commission to explore legal means of circumventing the Supreme Court ruling. A referendum was held in 1956, in which voters approved a limited constitutional convention where this would be addressed. The results would later be called the Stanley Plan. The Blacks of the state voted almost solidly against even holding the referendum. Dr. E.B. Henderson of Falls Church, vice president of the Virginia State Conference of the NAACP, reported that in nine Northern Virginia counties, Black citizens readily signed a statement opposing all forms of segregation in public life. He said that less than 1 percent of those asked refused to sign.[188] It was not stopped.

Governor Stanley summoned the Virginia Assembly into special session on August 27, 1956, and presented the Stanley Plan. It included a requirement that the governor close any schools under court order to integrate and cut off all state funding for any school that tried to open in compliance with the court order. Without state funds, the locality could neither try to operate integrated schools with its own funds nor close the schools and provide tuition grants for private schools, when available. No Black students entered a White school in Virginia during the 1956–57 school year.[189]

149

A month before, in July 1956, seeing this mass resistance movement, as it was called, gather steam under the governor and Senator Byrd's political clout, Delegate Catherine Stone of Arlington stated, "Academic arguments do not seem to change anyone's mind. I place great reliance on the ability of church leaders to affect a slow but more sure change in attitudes."[190]

As predicted, a group made up of local church leaders and likeminded citizens called the Fairfax County Council on Human Relations formed in February 1957 in response to the Stanley Plan. It stated in its *Congressional Christian Church of Fairfax County Newsletter*:

> *We are a democratic association of people who share the concern that those of different races, colors and creeds and other conditions of life should come to a better understanding of one another, based on a respect for the inherent worth and dignity of every individual. We believe unequivocally that every individual possesses the inalienable right as confirmed by the Bill of Rights in our Constitution to equal opportunity for the fullest development and use of his capacities. We recognize that legislation to safeguard this right can be fully effective only in an atmosphere of mutual understanding, trust, and respect.*[191]

The resistance continued. Eighteen months later, in August 1958, a statement by and with the names of forty-nine ministers of Fairfax County and Falls Church appeared in several newspapers, expressing opposition to enforcing segregation in the schools on the basis of race as well as all efforts to provide substitutes for the public school system. The statement was published in the *Northern Virginia Sun* on August 22, 1958; the *Washington Post and Times Herald* on August 23, 1958; the *Evening Star* on August 23, 1958; and the *Fairfax County Sun-Echo* on August 28, 1958.

At last, a court case was heard in the Virginia Supreme Court of Appeals brought on by these sentiments and lobbying efforts. On the nineteenth of January 1959, it outlawed school closings and ordered that the state must support public free schools, including those that were integrated. It nullified the Stanley Plan. By this time, Governor Stanley was out of office. The mass resistance movement ended.[192]

The racial desegregation of the public schools of Fairfax County was achieved by the closing of the all–African American schools and the busing of Black children to formerly all-White schools. Beginning in 1960, African American students were slowly admitted to White schools through a pupil placement application process.

Eleven Oaks Elementary School remained segregated until the school was closed in 1966.[193] In 2008, Eleven Oaks Elementary School was torn down.[194] Where the school once stood is only a memory. George Mason Boulevard runs through it. Homes have been built in the area.

The End of the School Street Community

The Farr family, commonwealth attorney Wilson M. Farr (1884–1959) and his sister-in-law Viola Orr, sold a 146-acre property to the Town of Fairfax in 1958. It was in turn proffered by the town to the University of Virginia to create a college branch in Northern Virginia. The college would later become independent of the University of Virginia and become George Mason University.[195] An important community between the new college, later university, and downtown Fairfax was the segregated School Street community. In addition, this community was also on a main thoroughfare, Chain Bridge Road, into town, where its homes, store and church were located. As the college expanded, it became a perfect location for new development.

As the city's first mayor, John C. Wood, said in 1962, "Fairfax has a wonderful past and present and an even greater future."[196]

George Mason College developers came calling first to homeowners closest to the campus on School Street. Below is a form letter prepared for residents in the 1960s. It was found in the John C. Wood papers at George Mason University.[197]

The Board of Control for Land Acquisition for George Mason College is presently undertaking necessary preliminary actions to acquire additional land for the College as jointly authorized by the Counties of Arlington and Fairfax and Falls Church.

In the process of planning for expansion of the College certain properties that are either contiguous, adjacent, or close to the existing site will be considered for purchase. A determination will subsequently be made as to the exact parcels of land that will be required for site expansion.

To assist the Board of Control in its selection of property to expand George Mason College, an appraisal of the property under consideration is presently being conducted by Mr. Guy C. McGee, a Member of Appraisal Institute. It is estimated this appraisal will be completed about May 1, 1967, and will serve to provide the basis for subsequent actions by the Board to designate the area for college acquisition and to acquire the property deemed necessary.

An examination of land parcels indicates that you are the owner of _____. This area is being considered for inclusion in the College land acquisition program. Sometime within the next 60 days you may be contacted and requested to discuss the sale of your property.

To provide a vehicle to administer the land acquisition program the Board of Control has designated a Coordinator to serve as a central and permanent clearing point for the property owners. If I can be of any assistance or provide you with additional information, please call me at 703-591-4600, George Mason College, 4400 University Drive, Fairfax, Virginia.

Very Truly yours,
R.H Pierce
Coordinator and Clerk of the Board

The Groomes family were neighbors to Etta Willson's family home on Chain Bridge Road. The home was not torn down when many in the community sold to a developer in 1989.
Photo courtesy of Jenee Lindner.

Every few years, as the university expanded, other developers came to call. The land around the campus became more valuable. In 1989, a land development company bought out thirty-five property owners and thirty acres of land in the School Street area. This would be the death blow for the heart of the community. Homeowners were courted by full homeowner value offers saying their property would be used for commercial George Mason University student housing and buildings. The residents already knew George Mason University could access their land through eminent domain from a letter sent to community members in 1967. Some neighbors had had to sell their homes and property through that process years before. After the buyout, the company announced that it "propos[ed] to build 240 units, filling the wooded land with luxury town houses and single-family houses that could sell for as much as $500,000 and would be marketed to young professionals."[198] Ultimately, this company did not built these units. Instead, it sold the land to another company, which developed the site in this very way. Both companies made quite a lot of money.[199] In hindsight, many families are still uneasy about the entire sequence of events. For them, this was home.[200]

Developers in 2000 and 2010 finally finished buying the remaining holdouts and the rest of the land, developing the rest of the community entirely.[201] Today, the community does not mirror in any way the past. It has apartments, luxury homes and townhouses, George Mason University satellite buildings, businesses, a retirement facility and a health clinic. There are a few homes left on West Drive and one home at 4300 Chain Bridge Road, Fairfax, Virginia—the old Groomes family house—which has been converted into the office for the Eaves by Avalon Apartment Living. The Mount Calvary Church at 4325 Chain Bridge Road, Fairfax, Virginia, and the presently empty Court House Market building across the street from the church are all that is left.

Chapter 4

TIMELINE OF BLACK LIVES
IN FAIRFAX, VIRGINIA

By Jenee Lindner

1683: Fitzhugh family land to create Ravensworth plantation

1783: Nicholas Fitzhugh at Ravensworth Plantation, east and south of downtown Fairfax, Virginia

1789: Richard Radcliffe moves with family to Mount Vineyard Plantation, west and north of Fairfax, including downtown Fairfax, Virginia

1800: Fairfax courthouse completed

1805: Town of Providence (Fairfax) established. Nicknamed Fairfax Courthouse

1802–1812: Little River Turnpike constructed

1820+: Jermantown Community is a multiculturally vibrant farming area with enslaved and freed

1850: William Fitzhugh's will frees his Ravensworth Plantation enslaved, twenty years after his death

1861–1865: American Civil War

1865: Freedmen Bureau established in Fairfax Courthouse

1866: First "Colored School" in Fairfax, Virginia opened

1868: Jermantown Cemetery founded

1868: Ilda Community created with purchase of five acres by Horace Gibson and his wife, Margaret Brooks. Moses Parker is his partner. They run a blacksmith and wheelwright on the Little River Turnpike

1870: Mount Calvary Baptist Church founded in School Street area

1874: Second "Colored School" opened to replace the first one, near Fairfax Memorial Cemetery on Main Street, walking distance between Jermantown and School Street communities (closes 1927)

1877: Horace Gibson's daughter Matilda Gibson marries Page Parker. Ilda Community is named after her

1878: Colored Methodist-Episcopal Church founded in School Street area (closed by 1820)

1889: New trustees for Jermantown Cemetery. Colbert/Payne families acquire large parcels of Jermantown.

1902: Virginia passed the first state constitution to require segregation. Jim Crow laws enacted. A local example is the Fairfax Railroad Station, which had separate "but equal" entrances.

1904: Trolley from Washington, D.C., to Fairfax. Patrons separated by race at the Virginia border after crossing the Potomac River. When it first started in 1896, this was not the case.

1909: NAACP founded with North Virginia chapter. Mission: To ensure the political, educational, social and economic equality of rights of all persons and to eliminate race-based discrimination

1927: Rosenwald School built and dedicated in School Street Community

Children in party hats on School Street in the 1960s. *Photo courtesy of Rita Colbert.*

1935: First African American grand jury in Fairfax County Circuit Court

1950s: New African American residences on School Street

May 1954: *Brown vs. Board of Education.* All Jim Crow laws formally ended.

September 1954–June 1965: Luther Jackson High School "for Negroes"

1953–1966: Eleven Oaks Public Elementary School replaced the Fairfax Rosenwald School

1961: Town of Fairfax becomes a city; matures into an urban village with a strong sense of community

1962: Jermantown annexed to Fairfax City. Eminent domain of residences to make commercial district.

1963: George Mason College (later University) main campus moved permanently to Fairfax, Virginia. It was founded in 1957.

1989–2010: School Street community sold by residents and acquired by the university and developers to create upscale townhouses, apartments, businesses, George Mason University satellite properties, etc.

PART III.

MAKING A DIFFERENCE

Chapter 1

JIM FERGUSON'S EATING HOUSE
AND LIVERY STABLES

By William Page Johnson II

Appeared in an earlier form in the Fare Facs Gazette, *the newsletter of Historic Fairfax City Inc.*

James Ferguson (a.k.a. Jim Fogg) was the son of John and Mary Ferguson. He was born in Fairfax County, about 1821. James Ferguson was first married to Nancy (last name unknown), born c. 1835.[202] The couple had seven known children, at least two of whom died in infancy.

During the Civil War, Jim was a hostler (a.k.a. groom) to Confederate general Joseph E. Johnston.[203] Jim had charge of Fannie, a bay mare thoroughbred and a favorite of the general.

On May 31, 1862, General Johnston was astride Fannie during the Battle of Seven Pines when he was struck in the right shoulder by a bullet, immediately followed by a shell fragment, which hit him in the chest. He tumbled from Fannie, unconscious, with a broken shoulder blade and two broken ribs. Fannie, however, was uninjured. In fact, Fannie survived many battles having never been wounded. She lived out her days on a Virginia farm.[204]

After the war, Jim Ferguson settled at Fairfax Court House. He operated Allison's Stables and an eating house. The structures stood on the east side of Mechanics Street (now University Drive), north of present-day Old Town Hall between Main and North Streets. The site now comprises a portion of Old Town Square.

Eating houses were the eighteenth- and nineteenth-century equivalent of today's restaurants and cafés. Although abundant in urban areas, such as nearby Alexandria and Washington, D.C., eating houses were not as

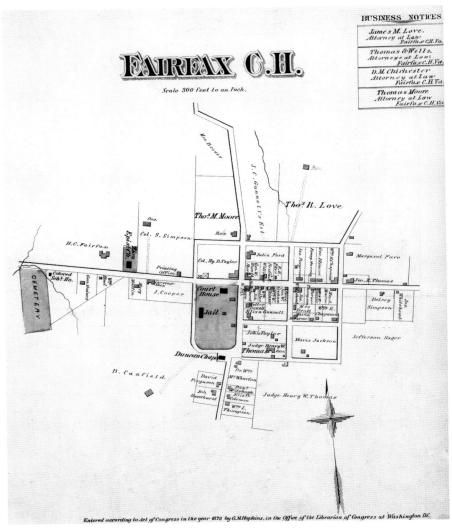

1878 Fairfax Town map. "Colored School" is on the left, next to the city cemetery. *Taken from G. M. Hopkins's* Atlas of Fifteen Miles Around Washington. *Library of Congress.*

common in rural areas. From 1869 to 1899 there was just one at Fairfax Court House: Ferguson's.

Start-up capital and overhead for an eating house were minimal. Advertising was also unnecessary, as these places were known intimately and frequented mainly by locals. Most proprietors of eating houses operated

Animals on Fairfax's Main Street in 1910. The *Fairfax Herald* often complained about the barking of dogs at night and pigs running free. There were lots of animals around. Opening the window at night for breezes ushered in a symphony of noises—not always welcomed. *From* This Was Virginia 1900–1927 as Shown by Glass Negatives of J. Harry Shannon, the Rambler, *compiled by Connie and Mayo Stuntz. Courtesy of Virginia Room, Fairfax County Public Library.*

their businesses from their homes. Thus, the eating house contained much of the personality and temperament of the owner.

Although not exclusively operated by African Americans, in the segregated South, eating houses were one of the few business opportunities available to former slaves. However, if not as owners, the presence of African Americans in eating houses was ubiquitous, as cooks or waiters. This was certainly the case in the South immediately after the Civil War. Newly freed slaves had, after all, performed these duties in bondage for generations.

However, while African Americans might have owned eating houses, they were likely not allowed to dine in them—unless, of course, the eating house catered exclusively to other African Americans. Segregation encompassed all facets of life in America, particularly in the South, including eating houses. Jim Ferguson's Eating House was segregated and catered exclusively to White customers.

Jim's Ferguson's business was well known and very successful. He was even known to cater a few events:

Local Affairs. Masonic Supper—A supper will be given at Fairfax C.H. in the Masonic Hall at the next regular communication Dec., 18, to J. Y. Worthington, in consideration of his valuable services as Worshipful Master of Henry Lodge No. 57 A.F.A.M. A full attendance of the members, is desired.

James Furguson [sic]*, caterer.*[205]

By the 1870s, Ferguson's Eating House was a well-established landmark at Fairfax Court House. In 1874, the following appeared in the *Alexandria Gazette*:

James Ferguson, (who was a hostler to Gen. J.E. Johnston during the war), a colored man whose house is much resorted to on public days by white people, as Jim keep an excellent table and an orderly, respectable house.[206]

Years after relocating to Florida, John Lee McWhorter, associate editor of the *Tampa Tribune* and former resident of Fairfax Court House, fondly recalled Fairfax and Jim Ferguson's in an editorial:

Back in our boyhood days in Virginia there were four great court weeks a year and Monday in each of those weeks was known as "Sale Day." It was the day when all the fine stock, horses, cattle, sheep and hogs to be disposed of at more than usual farm price, were bought and auctioned. It was a big day with the farmers; for, despite the fact that whiskey was plentiful and cheap, and there was usually fighting from the "court house" to "Jim Fogg's" restaurant half a mile down the street, these sales days were in reality "fair" days for the county. Great exhibitions of fine stock for breeding purposes was especially the purpose of the exhibitors, and of course there was always a great amount of stock sold.[207]

The monthly (and special quarterly) sessions of the court...provided opportunities to transact all manner of public business—from issuing licenses and collecting taxes to hearing litigation and holding elections. They were also social events and market days; there people came to meet their friends, hear the news, see who came circuit-riding with the justices, sell their produce, and buy what they needed.[208]

Jim Ferguson was enumerated in the U.S. Census of 1880 as a resident of Fairfax Court House, race "mulatto," age fifty, occupation "Keeps Eating House." Living in his household were his wife, Nancy, age forty-five; daughter Alice, age eighteen; son Royal, age fourteen; son Edward, age twelve; son Shelly, age eleven; and son Joseph, age four. Also living in the household as a boarder was Addie Ware, race "mulatto," age nineteen, occupation "School Teacher."

Nancy Ferguson died sometime between 1880 and 1887. On November 13, 1887, James, then a widower, married Susan Jackson in Fairfax County. Susan was born in March 1849 and was a native of Madison County, Virginia.

In 1886, Albert A. Dewey brought suit in Fairfax County Circuit Court against James Ferguson for the nonpayment of a $90 debt. To secure Dewey, the Fairfax County Circuit Court ordered Ferguson's property to be sold at auction. On March 17, 1890, Mary C. Watkins was the high bidder at $480.[209] The property was transferred to her by deed in 1891.[210]

> The house and lot at Fairfax C.H. owned and occupied for many years as a house of private entertainment by James Ferguson (colored) otherwise known as Jim Fogg, was sold on Monday to Mary C. Watkins for $480.[211]

It is highly probable that Jim Ferguson continued to operate his eating house and the livery stable as the tenant of Mary Watkins after losing the property. The following is a description of an eating house at Fairfax Court House from a traveler in 1892:

> We adjourned to a pleasant house, where we had a dinner for twenty-five cents that, if persisted in, would put meat a foot thick on a stone statue. Pork and turnips, corn bread and sweet potatoes, preserves and cream and honey, homemade white bread, yellow butter, rich milk, beefsteak, and potatoes, pickles and plenty, and a good-looking woman with a melodious voice to wait on us and watch over us.[212]

In 1898, Mary Watkins sold her property, including Ferguson's old eating house and stables, to Colonel Joseph Willard.[213]

> Mr. Joseph E. Willard has purchased the lot at Fairfax Courthouse on which are situated the house and stables used by James Ferguson for many years as an eating house and livery stables. It is said he expects soon to have them torn down.[214]

With the loss and subsequent demolition of their old eating house and stable, Jim and Susan Ferguson were forced to relocate nearby. On July 26,

1899, Susan Ferguson purchased a near half-acre of Lot No. 15 on the south side of Main Street for $850 from George H. Carroll[215] of Washington, D.C.[216] George H. Carroll had acquired the property from the estate of Narcissa Monroe in 1886. George H. Carroll was the son of Susan Carroll, and both were the former slaves of Narcissa Monroe.[217] The lot purchased by Susan Ferguson extended from the intersection of Main and East Streets, west along Main Street for 136 feet and south along East Street for 134 feet. Excluded from the purchase was a small 30-by-134-foot lot on the western border of Lot No. 15, which had been acquired by Susan A. Davis in 1893.[218] James and Susan Ferguson mortgaged $550 for the purchase. The "two story frame and shingle" dwelling was insured for $550.[219]

The U.S. Census of 1900 provides additional insight into the life and habits of Jim Ferguson. He was then a prisoner in the Fairfax County jail. The census enumerates his birth as October 1821, thus making him then seventy-eight years old. His occupation of "Eating House Keeper" is also recorded. The census indicated he owned his home. Jim may have been in the Fairfax County Jail for selling liquor, a charge he faced several times during his lifetime.[220] Susan Ferguson, age fifty-one, "Eating House Keeper," is also listed in the same census. Enumerated with her is her son Shell, age thirty, born in Virginia in April 1870, occupation "Day laborer." Also listed is her grandson Wyatt Ferguson, age ten, born in Washington, D.C., in May 1890, occupation "At School."

Susan Ferguson died on March 19, 1901.[221] The appearance of her brief obituary in the *Fairfax Herald* gives some indication as to her value and standing in the community.

In addition to the mortgage, Susan Ferguson's estate was indebted to Oliver Bishop "O.B." Campbell & Co., General Merchandise; Dr. Walker Peyton Moncure, MD; and James W. Taylor, Undertaker. The estate was placed in the hands of a "receiver," Fairfax County sheriff George A. Gordon. As the receiver, Gordon's job was to seize the assets of Ferguson and, if possible, collect rents from the occupants. Fairfax attorney Robert W. Moore, of the firm Moore & Keith,[222] wrote to creditor George H. Carroll on the matter in October 1903:

> *The Receiver has not been able to collect rent from old Jim Ferguson, except a very small amount, and there has been no chance to rent to anyone else.*[223]

Dr. Moncure, who had attended both Susan and her son Royal Ferguson between 1900 and 1901, filed an itemized bill with the Fairfax County

Circuit Court for his services. This bill implies that Royal Ferguson may have died in late 1900, when the billings by Dr. Moncure for him ceased. If so, Royal was followed in death by his mother, Susan, who died in March 1901. Royal's wife, "the prepossessing,"[224] Matilda Ferguson, was apparently also living in the household, as she is credited with paying rent to Sheriff Gordon from October 1903 until May 1904. Subsequently, the Fergusons may have been evicted by Sheriff Gordon, as a new tenant, Kate Murray, is credited with paying the rent from May 1904 until September 1905.

In November 1905, Susan and Jim Ferguson's property was advertised and ordered sold by the court to meet their obligations. Oliver B. Campbell was the purchaser.

> *Wednesday, November 1, 1905…Half an Acre. Said lot is improved by a good FRAM[E] DWELLING HOUSE and Stable. It is the same lot which was formerly owned by Harrison Monroe, and later by George Carroll, who sold it to the late Susan Ferguson. This is a valuable piece of property. About ten electric trains per day connect the Town of Fairfax with Washington, D.C.*[225]

The last known reference to Jim Ferguson was in May 1904, when he paid partial rent to Sheriff Gordon on his former home.[226] He would have then been eighty-three years old. Nothing further is known about him.

At least one of his children survived him. Sheldon Ferguson was employed as a waiter in Washington, D.C., and a butler in New York City in 1920.[227]

Chapter 2

FIRST BLACK GRAND JURY
IN FAIRFAX COUNTY, 1935

By Jenee Lindner

Colored Grand Jury

For the first time in more than a half century, a special grand jury of colored men sat in the Fairfax Circuit Court Friday last and returned true bills against E. Louise Carpenter, and her daughter Mary Carpenter, colored, on presentments for arson. It was in this case that a regular grand jury, composed of white returned true bills. On motion of counsel for the defendants, that the jury returned the indictment had no colored men on it, and that the list from which it was drawn contained the names of no colored men, Judge McCarthy set aside the indictment and ordered a new jury. This was composed of Alexander White of Sideburn, foreman; Attana [Atana] Payne, John Pearson and Henry Page, of Fairfax; Ollie Tinner and Otis Wade, Falls Church, and James [Joseph] Collins, Merrifield.

—Fairfax Herald, *May 31, 1935*

In 1935, a jury was established in Fairfax County with African American members. This was significant because Blacks were usually excluded from serving on juries in Virginia. Press reports indicated that these were the first African Americans to serve on a Fairfax County jury since 1883.

Exclusion of African Americans from juries because of their race was unconstitutional and could result in miscarriages of justice. In this case, an

First Black Fairfax County circuit court jury, 1935. *Left to right, top row*: Ollie Tinner (Falls Church), Alexander White (Sideburn), John Pearson (Fairfax), Henry Page (Fairfax); *bottom row*: Otis Wade (Falls Church), Joseph Collins, misidentified in newspaper articles as "James Collins" (Merrifield), Atana Payne (Fairfax, son of Reverend Benjamin Payne). *Courtesy of Virginia Room, Fairfax County Public Library.*

all-Black grand jury was established after protests from an attorney defending two African American women accused of arson.[228]

Each man chosen for the Fairfax County jury was well respected. The jurors were drawn from the membership of the Fairfax County Colored Citizens Association. This organization was founded in September 1928. Its purposes were multifold for the benefit of Black lives, their families and their livelihoods in Fairfax County, Virginia. Several voices are better than one when requesting a change. In 1941, the association's *Thirteenth Anniversary Achievement Report* (which was compiled by one of the jurors, publicity manager Ollie Tinner) stated:[229]

WATCHWORDS: Vigilance, Progress, Cooperation

PURPOSE: To organize the Negroes in Fairfax County, Virginia for the purpose of voting in all elections.
AIMS: To better Negro citizenship in Fairfax County through its stand for:

A. FULLER USE OF THE BALLOT BY ALL NEGROES
B. GREATER IMPROVEMENT IN COLORED SCHOOLS
C. JUSTICE IN THE COURTS AND PUBLIC CONVEYANCES
D. ACTIVE PARTICIPATION IN ALL COUNTY AND CIVIC AFFAIRS
E. PROMOTION OF A BETTER FEELING BETWEEN THE RACES
F. BOOSTING THE COUNTY AS A DESIRABLE PLACE TO LIVE

ACHIEVEMENT: …Protested to the authorities (May, 1934) about the established practice of excluding Negroes from all juries [in] Fairfax County. May 24, 1935—the first Negroes to serve on the jury in Fairfax County were drawn from our association. These members were Alexander L. White, foreman, Sideburn, Va.; Otis Wade, Falls Church; Atana Payne, Fairfax; John R. Pearson, Fairfax; Joseph Collins, Merrifield; Henry Page, Fairfax; and Ollie W. Tinner, Falls Church. [230]

In the 1935 Carpenter case, these new jurors came to the same conclusion as the previous jury: guilty as charged for arson. [231]

Alexander Lawrence White (1881–1947) was the court case foreman. He was a Washington, D.C. office clerk and by 1930 a farmer and clerk for the Farm and Forest Services Industries from Sideburn, south of Fairfax, Virginia. His wife, Nellie, was a U.S. Department of Agriculture clerk. [232] In 1940, they owned their own home and 100 acres in Sideburn and had no children. [233] In 1964, now with 150 acres, his widow sold to developers where Sideburn Avenue runs through their land today with 50 acres on one side and 100 acres on the other side. [234]

Simon Atana Payne (1897–1978): The next chapter will discuss him at length. He was a good man who for many years worked as a chauffeur for the McCandlish family in Fairfax and drove the school bus for Black students and who wanted a high school education at the Industrial School for Colored Youth in Manassas, Virginia. He and his wife, Virginia Conic Payne, were the proud parents of seven children: Dora, William (Sonny), Carrie, Thomas, Nettie, Harold and Lynwood.

Mah 24, 1935.

State Comptroller has stated that he does not feel authorized to pay more than
$3.00 per day for such accommodations, that being the rate charged for State
prisoners by certain hospitals in Virginia; and it further appearing to the Court
that this was an emergency case and that under the circumstances hereinabove
mentioned it was necessary and proper in order to safeguard the health and life
of said prisoner that he be sent to said Georgetown University Hospital without
delay, and that the bill of $68.00 is a reasonable one and should be allowed;

Upon consideration whereof the Court doth now adjudge and order that the said
bill of Georgetown University Hospital be, and the same hereby is, allowed, and
ordered certified to the State Comptroller for payment, forthwith, together with
a copy of this order.

//

IN THE CIRCUIT COURT OF FAIRFAX COUNTY, VIRGINIA.

VIRGINIA PUBLIC SERVICE CO.,
A Corporation,
            Plaintiff
      v.
J. SINCLAIR RECTOR,
            Defendant

                    AT LAW

                    O R D E R

                    May Term, 1935.

On motion of the Defendant, and with the consent of the Plaintiff, it is
ordered that the Defendant be and he hereby is given the right to withdraw the
plea of recoupment and counterclaim heretofore filed by the Defendant.

//

It is this day ordered by the Court that the SPECIAL GRAND JURY OF INQUEST
in and for the body of the County of Fairfax, Virginia, at this term of the
Court, shall consist of seven (7) persons.

The following named persons who were selected and summoned in the mode
prescribed by law under the authority of a writ of venire facias issued by the
Clerk of this Court on the 20th day of May, 1935, and directed to and delivered
to the Sheriff of this County, and being executed and now returned to the Court
so endorsed, and is received and filed, to appear here today, at this term of
the court, and serve as Grand Jurors on the Special Grand Jury of Inquest in
and for the body of the County of Fairfax, Virginia, this day appeared agreeably
to said summons, to-wit:

          1. JOHN PEARSON   2. OLLIE TINNER
          3. OTIS WADE   4. ATANNA PAYNE
          5. JOSEPH E. COLLINS   6. HENRY PAGE
                  7. ALEXANDER WHITE

AND were empanelled according to law, and having had the usual and requisite
questions put to each of them, were all found to be qualified and competent Grand
Jurors according to the Statute. Thereupon, ALEXANDER WHITE was selected by the
Court as the Foreman of the said Grand Jury, and was sworn as such in the mode
prescribed by law, and each of said Grand Jurors was sworn as such in the mode
prescribed by law, and having received their charge from the Court, they retired
to their room to consider of their presentments and indictments, and after a
while returned into open Court with the following indictments, to-wit:-

An indictment in the name of the Commonwealth of Virginia vs. L. LOUISE
CARPENTER, for felonious arson, endorsed, "A True Bill, Alexander L. White,
Foreman".

An indictment in the name of the Commonwealth of Virginia vs. MARY LUCY
CARPENTER, for felonious arson, endorsed "A True Bill Alexander L. White,
Foreman"

May 24, 1935. Jury names in court order. *Fairfax Minutes Book 17, p. 79. Courtesy of Fairfax Circuit Court Historic Records Center.*

May 20, 1935.

| Commonwealth of Virginia)
vs.
L. LOUISE CARPENTER) | Upon an INDICTMENT of the Grand Jury for feloniously procuring destruction of dwelling house with intent to injure insurer. |

and

| Commonwealth of Virginia)
vs.
MARY LUCY CARPENTER) | Upon an INDICTMENT of the Grand Jury for felonious arson |

This day came the defendants, L. Louise Carpenter and Mary Lucy Carpenter, each in person and by counsel, and moved the Court to quash the two indictments returned against L. Louise Carpenter, one charging felonious arson, and the other charging her with feloniously procuring destruction of dwelling house with intent to injure insurer, and the indictment against the said Mary Lucy Carpenter, charging her with felonious arson upon the ground that no members of the colored or Negro race served upon the Grand Jury which returned said indictments, and that it was not customary to call members of said colored or Negro race for said Grand Jury service, which motion the Court grants in accordance with the decision of the Supreme Court of the United States in the "Scottsboro Cases" and quashes the said three indictments against the said L. Louise Carpenter and Mary Lucy Carpenter.
//

It is this day ordered by the Court that the Clerk of this Court do issue a writ of venire facias for a special Grand Jury of Inquest in and for the body of the County of Fairfax, commanding the Sheriff thereof to summon seven (7) persons, of the colored, or Negro race, of this county, from a list to be furnished by the Judge of this Court, naming the persons to be so summoned, to appear here on Friday, May 24, 1935, at 10 O'clock A. M., and serve as Grand Jurors on the Special Grand Jury of Inquest in and for the body of said County, this being the first Colored Grand Jury summoned in the history of this County so far as now known.
//

B. F. MILLER, who was heretofore granted a license to celebrate the Rites of Matrimony within the limits of the Commonwealth of Virginia, and executed a bond and took the oath prescribed by law in the penalty of $500, with E. H. Jones as his justified surety and the said E. H. Jones having departed this life, he now executes a new bond in the penalty of $500.00, conditioned as the law directs together with J. W. Pobst as his justified surety.
//

 Fee $1.50 The Inventory and Appraisement of the estate of MARTHA A. SHERMAN, deceased, was received, endorsed approved by the Commissioner of Accounts, and ordered to be recorded.
//

IN THE CIRCUIT COURT FOR FAIRFAX COUNTY, VIRGINIA

Commonwealth of Virginia

Vs.

Allen C. Cornwell

This matter is heard this 20th day of May, 1935, upon motion of the said Allen C. Cornwell to be discharged from custody for non-payment of fine and costs. The Attorney for the Commonwealth having been given due notice of this

May 20, 1935. Commonwealth of Virginia vs. L. Louise Carpenter and Mary Lucy Carpenter. Courtesy of Fairfax Circuit Court Historic Records Center.

John R. Pearson (1871–after 1950):[235] In 1929, he was appointed as a Fairfax Courthouse janitor.[236] His proximity to the judges in the court and his exemplary character probably influenced his appointment to the Black jury of 1935. He was born in Fairfax, Virginia, and was from the Zion Street area. He was a grandson to Francis Coffer IV (of the founding Coffer family of Burke, Virginia) and son of Charles Pearson and Sarah (one of four Coffer-Pearsons of Burke).[237] In the 1940 census, John Pearson is listed as sixty-nine years old, living on a Payne Street (now called Chain Bridge Road) side street with no name. He was still a janitor, probably for the Fairfax Courthouse. He owned his home. The census includes his wife, Jane Pearson, age sixty-two; daughter Beatrice Pearson (Gartrell), age thirty-seven; son-in-law Bernard Gartrell, age thirty-five; daughter Virginia Burkes, age thirty-six; son-in-law Charles Burkes, age thirty-seven; granddaughter Doris Burkes, age fifteen; grandson Kenneth Burkes, age eight; grandson Bernard Gartrell, age nine; and grandson Robert Gartrell, age six.[238] In the 1950 census, John has his last name misspelled "Pierson." He is listed as seventy-nine years old and not able to work. Again, he lived with his wife, Janie L. Pierson, age seventy-two, and two daughters with their families. The last names for each of their families are listed as Burke and Hartvell.[239]

Otis Richard Wade (1886–1940) was born in Frederick County, Maryland, but lived most of his life in Falls Church, Virginia. In the 1920 census, he is listed as a janitor for an office building and owned his own home.[240] In the 1930 census, he is a "Laborer/Salary Worker" on a private estate (perhaps Layton Hall Estate in Fairfax, Virginia, owned by the politically influential Joseph Willard Jr. family). Interestingly, Otis Wade never went to school and could not read or write.[241] All others on the Black jury could.

Otis Wade owned half of a lot in Falls Church, Virginia. In 1939, along with several others, Wade was accused of delinquency of property tax in the local *News-Observer* newspaper.

> *On Monday, December 11th, 1939, in the front of the Court House door of Fairfax County, 12 noon, I will offer for sale the real estate belonging to the delinquent taxpayers for the year, 1937, unless the amount for which said lands are delinquent, together with delinquent interest and costs and charges shall, have been paid to the Treasurer, a description of which shall be seen in the Office of the Clerk of the Circuit Court. V. L. M. COYNER, Treasurer of Fairfax County, Virginia.[242]*

The amount he owed was $11.45. Publicizing people's tax debts was often used as part of a revenue-generating tactic, to take ownership of a property and sell it at auction to increase the government's revenue. This was done by many local governments in the South if taxes were not paid promptly.

Wade must have paid his debt, because he and his family were still living in Falls Church in the 1940 census, the year of his death.[243]

Otis Wade's obituary:

> *Passed at his residence. Loving son of Andrew Wade and the late Jane Wade. Survived by his devoted wife Martha T. Wade, son Otis Wade, Jr; daughter, Edith Wade; 2 sisters; two brothers; 3 grandchildren, other relatives and friends. John T. Rhines funeral home in charge of services. Funeral was held at the Second Baptist Church, Falls Church, Rev. Costner, officiating. Interment Church cemetery.*[244]

Joseph Collins (1886–1945) was born on April 14, 1886, and was the third son of William Collins Sr. and the second child of Mariah Fish-Collins. He married Annie Blackwell, the daughter of Eli Blackwell and Mary Tyler, but the couple had no children of their own. They tried to adopt a son early on in their marriage but returned him to the orphanage. After Joseph's brother Norman was tragically killed, Joseph and Annie became legal guardians of his orphaned daughters Aileen and Thelma.[245] Joseph worked at the Rosslyn Gas Company in Arlington along with his brothers Bud (William Jr.) and Norman and his nephew Guy. He purchased many parcels of land in and around the "Pines" and Merrifield. Joseph and Annie became deacons at the First Baptist Church of Merrifield and remained dedicated and devoted until their deaths. Joseph Collins died in church of a massive heart attack on July 23, 1945.[246]

The small community of Merrifield did not have an increase in its Black population until the 1900s, when the area known as the Pines was developed. A search of land deeds within the county shows that the earliest resident within this Black community was William H. Collins Jr., who purchased his land in 1905.[247] Other families purchased property once the Collins brothers had established themselves.[248]

Henry Page (June 2, 1878–March 28, 1947) was born in Loudoun County, Virginia, before moving to Fairfax City. He and his wife, Aurelia Elizabeth Horton Page (1885–January 25, 1948), had a total of thirteen children. Their names were Clarington, Maud, Grace, Elenora, Henrietta, Rosemond,

William, Clarence, Bessie, Lottie, Lester, Otis Nathanial and Marie. They all grew to adulthood.[249] By the 1930 census, Henry owned his large home, field and garden.

Page was listed as a salary worker in private work and as having completed two years of college. In the 1930 census, his wife and children are listed: Aurelia Page, age forty-nine; Etta Page, age twenty-two; William Page, age twenty; Clarence Page, age eighteen; Bessie Page, age sixteen; Lottie Page, age thirteen; Leslie Page, age nine; and Marie Page, age seven.[250] Per the 1940 census, they had living with them two sons, two daughters, a son-in-law, a grandson and two granddaughters.[251]

Ollie Tinner (1899–1964) was born in Falls Church, Virginia, on July 26, 1899. His grandfather was Charles Tinner (1847–1917), a well-known Falls Church community member. On his emancipation, Charles Tinner and his wife, Mary Elizabeth, temporarily rented a home but soon bought some land and constructed a brick home for their growing family in Falls Church, Virginia, just across the river from Washington, D.C.

Charles was a talented stonemason—something in great demand in the area, including in Washington, D.C. He also earned a good living from the stone quarry he bought with several of his sons, including Joseph Tinner (1877–1928). The entire area was later called Tinner Hill. The Tinner family quarried pink granite rock at the base of Tinner Hill from the late 1800s into the 1920s.[252] The parents also subdivided the land, once part of a tobacco plantation, into ten home lots, one for each of their children.[253] Tripp, a prominent White farmer after the Civil War, sold this land to the Tinner family.[254]

THE TINNER HILL COMMUNITY has been recognized as being the location where the first rural branch of the National Association for the Advancement of Colored People (NAACP) was initiated in the United States. In 1915, a few brave African American citizens—led by E.B. Henderson and his neighbor Joseph Tinner—fought a proposed ordinance that would have segregated housing. They called themselves the Colored Citizens Protective League (CCPL). The group evolved to become the first rural branch of the NAACP in the nation in 1918.[255]

Like those of his ancestors before him, Ollie Tinner's life was full of hard work and service to his fellow men. His focus was the education of children and church stewardship. Ollie graduated from Armstrong High School in

Washington, D.C., in 1919.[256] He would receive a four-year college degree, as well. Deacon Ollie William Tinner, as he was later called, was a teacher for many years.[257]

After World War II, improvements of schools for the Black children of Fairfax County was one of the goals of the Fairfax County branch of the NAACP. An interracial committee was formed to work with citizens and school administrators for a Black high school within the county. Ollie was a member of that committee. At that time, Black children of high school age were either being bussed to the nearby Manassas Industrial School for Colored Youth or attending District of Columbia high schools. Later, Luther Jackson High School would be open for Black students in Fairfax County in 1954.[258]

Ollie married deaconess Etta W. Tinner and was a beloved father of one daughter, Mrs. Mildred T. Leak, a son-in-law and two grandchildren at the time of his death. He died on September 27, 1964, age sixty-five, in Alexandria City, Virginia, and was buried at the Second Baptist Church Cemetery.[259]

Chapter 3

SIMON ATANA PAYNE (1897–1978):
EDUCATING BY EXAMPLE

By Etta Willson, Rita Colbert, Linneall Naylor,
Rondia Prescott and Jenee Lindner

Atana Payne was my uncle (my mother's brother).
Also, he is related to Linneall Naylor.
—*Etta Willson*

Simon Atana Payne was buried at Pleasant Valley Memorial Park:
Gooding Family Cemetery at 8412 Little River Turnpike, Annandale,
Fairfax, Virginia. His parents were Reverend Benjamin Payne and Martha
Tibbs Payne, another ancestor discussed in this book. His relatives and
contributions extended to all those buried at Jermantown Cemetery,
including his children. Therefore, he is included here by the Jermantown
Cemetery descendants.

His obituary is shared by his last living child, Lynwood Payne. It states,

S.A. Payne, 80, Chairman of Mount Calvary Baptist Church: Simon
Atana Payne, 80, a lifelong resident of Fairfax who worked as a houseman
and chauffeur there until his retirement in 1972. He died of cancer at
Commonwealth Doctors hospital, December 9, 1978.

Mr. Payne, called Atana, was involved in community and church
activities most of his life. He was one of the first blacks to serve on a
Fairfax County grand jury. During the 1930s, in addition to his regular
job, he drove a bus to transport black children to and from the Manassas
Regional High School, then that area's only high school for blacks. Mr.
Payne would leave his home at 4:30 AM each school day, pick up children

Left: Atana Payne as a chauffeur. *Photo courtesy of Rita Colbert.*

Right: Virginia Conic Payne. *Photo courtesy of Rita Colbert.*

from black communities in Gum Springs, Falls Church, Centreville, and Fairfax, and drop them off at the high school. He then would work his regular job, returning to Manassas afterward to take the students back home. The son of a minister, Mr. Payne had been a member of Mount Calvary Baptist Church in Fairfax since 1925. Since 1930, he has served as chairman of the board at the church. He is a member of the church choir and served as superintendent of the Sunday school.

Survivors include his wife of 57 years, the former Virginia Conic, of the home; seven children, Dora P. Folks (deceased), William (Sunny) [Payne], and Carrie P.[ayne] Allen, both Falls Church; Thomas Randolph [Payne], and Nettie P.[ayne] Smith, both of Fairfax; Harold Lloyd [Payne], of Gunston, VA; and Lynwood Conic [Payne], also of the home; 42 grandchildren and 28 great grandchildren.

Atana Payne; his wife, Virginia; and their family all worked for years for country lawyer Fairfax Sheild McCandlish Sr. (1881–1934) and Mary Legrand Donohoe McCandlish, known as "Bam" (1888–1986). They had three children: Mary (married name Livingston; 1914–2007), Nancy

Clockwise from top left: Dora Payne Folks; William Payne; Thomas Payne, Carrie Lee Payne Allen. *Photos courtesy of Rita Colbert.*

Top, left: Nettie Payne Smith; *top, right*: Harold Payne; *bottom*: Lynwood Payne and his wife, Jeanette. *Photos courtesy of Rita Colbert.*

(married name Prichard; 1916–2006) and Fairfax "Sheild" Jr. (1918–2007). Mary McCandlish was widowed and in a wheelchair for many years. Her nickname, Bam, came to be because of a grandchild. Atana was Bam's assistant, friend, chauffeur and caregiver, especially after the early death of her husband.[260]

The Payne family and the McCandlish family were tightly overlapping over a lifetime together. Atana Payne's smoked hams, smoked in the backyard, were legendary. His wife, Virginia, worked in the kitchen as a great cook. Lynwood Payne remembers, as a teenager, the hot days of lawn mowing.[261]

Tom Prichard, a grandson to Mr. and Mrs. McCandlish, said,

> *Our family lived near Grandma Bam, who owned the Moore House where the Hamrock Restaurant is located today at 3950 Chain Bridge Road, Fairfax, Virginia. It used to be surrounded in the back by a lovely garden, grass and meadows. This site was known for their beautiful hydrangeas. Atana Payne's connection began on my grandparents' wedding day in 1911. He would often babysit me and my siblings. He was wonderful to us.*
>
> *My entire extended family observed through the years that Mr. Payne had another more important job—a labor of love really. He arose early in the morning before his work with us and after work did not return home until late at night. During that time, Atana Payne took African American high school age children back and forth to the Manassas Industrial School for Colored Youth in neighboring Prince William County. He would pick up students all over the county and return them home, twice a day, five days a week.*[262]

The only choices in Fairfax County for African Americans to attend high school were in Washington, D.C., including Dunbar High School, Phelps Vocational Center, Cardoza High School and Armstrong High School.[263] Or you could—hopefully—be transported to Prince William County to the Manassas Industrial School for Colored Youth.[264] This is why Mr. Payne decided he had to help and became their bus driver.

There was a very interesting *Fairfax Times* article written about the McCandlish and Payne families called "Two Families Reflect Two Histories," by Frank Mustac.[265] The Payne family worked for the McCandlish family for generations. A deep friendship was developed as they crisscrossed their long lives together. The following generations of McCandlishes would include the Prichards, the Livingstons and the Petersens. They, too, would be blessed to have the Payne family, especially Simon Atana Payne, in their lives.

Two Families Reflect Two Histories: Long Bloodlines Weave Road to Fairfax City's Past, Future
By Frank Mustac, Fairfax Times
February 24, 2005

Asked why they chose to live and stay in the City of Fairfax, many residents often cite the relatively low real estate tax rate, the good schools and amenities like the parks and the popular annual festivals.

Others say it is family that has kept them around, and, in the City of Fairfax, more than a few bloodlines run quite deep with roots that trace back for decades, some even for centuries.

One of the oldest families in the city's history is the Moore family. Among their descendants are the Petersens.

J. Chapman "Chap" Petersen, 36, Fairfax City resident and current member of the Virginia House of Delegates representing Fairfax, is part of the eighth generation of progeny to have come down from Fairfax Baptist preacher Jeremiah Moore.

Primarily due to his anti-establishment doctrine, Moore came into conflict with authorities during the late 18th century and was charged with preaching without a license in 1773. He ultimately regained his legal right to perform marriages in 1785.

Three generations later, R. Walton Moore, perhaps one of the most celebrated of the Moores, was born in 1859.

"We called him Uncle Walton," said Mary Petersen, 56, Moore's great-grandniece and Chap Petersen's mother.

An attorney by training, Moore was appointed Assistant Secretary of State by President Franklin Roosevelt in 1933, was made counselor to the president in 1937 and served in that post until he died in 1941.

A friend and confidant of the president, Moore often hosted Roosevelt at his home in Fairfax City, now called the Moore-McCandlish House, at 3950 Chain Bridge Road.

A great proponent of aviation while in its infancy, Moore knew the famous pilot and aviator Charles Lindbergh, who once took Mary Petersen's mother, Mary Walton McCandlish Livingston, for an airplane ride when she was 12 in 1926.

"Uncle Walton offered [family members] *tremendous windows to the world," Petersen said. "He was certainly the family leader."*

One of the more celebrated women in the Moore family was Petersen's grandmother, Mary LeGrand Donohoe McCandlish (1888–1986), affectionately known as Bam by her grandchildren.

Soon after she was born at what is now called the Fabio House at 3920 Chain Bridge Road, Bam's mother died from infection and the infant was carried to the Moore-McCandlish House to be raised by her uncle, R. Walton Moore, and his three unmarried sisters.

"My grandmother was really raised by [Uncle Walton] as his daughter," Petersen said.

Following her marriage to Fairfax Shields McCandlish, the son of Confederate Civil War officer and Pickett's Charge survivor Robert McCandlish, Bam moved to a house she and her husband built at what is now 3820 Chain Bridge Road.

Their wedding was held at the rebuilt Zion Church, now Truro, with a reception at Old Town Hall.

"She was a kind of vivid Southern woman that was the glue that kept the family together," Petersen said. "She was an incredibly hospitable person."

She never held a job or drove a car, Petersen said, but was very involved in community service...and was especially interested in George Mason University, sponsoring one of the first scholarships there.

"She [also] loved politics," Petersen said.

In the first election following passage of the 19th amendment in 1920 granting women the right to vote, Bam cast her vote early in the morning when the polls opened. Petersen said her grandmother jokingly told her she did so just in case she "had a stroke or got run over by a bus."

"Family always came first for her," she said. "There was a tremendous feeling of clan."

"There is this depiction of Southern women as shrinking violets, but they were very strong and vivid people," she said. "She represents something you don't see in the history books."

THE PAYNE FAMILY

Less than a mile south of the Moore-McCandlish House along Chain Bridge Road, in what was then primarily an African-American community, lived Simon Atana Payne in a house on West [Drive] with his wife, Virginia, and their seven children: Dora, William, Carrie Lee, Nettie, Thomas, Harold and Lynwood.

Payne was the son of Baptist preacher Benjamin Payne, who had a nearly five-acre farm on land now part of Fair Oaks Mall off Route 50 in Fairfax.

A chauffeur and cook for R. Walton Moore and the Moore family during a good part of his life, Payne, who died in 1978, was a longtime trustee and chairman of the deacon board at Mount Calvary Baptist Church at 4325 Chain Bridge Road in Fairfax City. At the church, he also served as superintendent of the Sunday school and was a member of the choir.

In 1935, Payne was one of seven blacks selected to sit on the first all-black grand jury empaneled in Fairfax County in the 20th century. During this time of racial segregation, an all-white grand jury had previously indicted a black woman and her daughter in a case of arson. Defense for the women complained that the jury that had issued the indictment contained no blacks, so a judge ordered a new jury, which included Payne.

All the African-American members on that jury were well-respected men in the community, said Payne's son, Thomas Payne, 70, a lifelong resident of Fairfax City.

"They were all well respected by whites and blacks," he said.

In addition to his work, his church duties and time with his family, Simon Atana Payne during the late 1940s and early 1950s drove a school bus that took students, including some of his own children, to Manassas Regional High School, a segregated all-black vocational school in Prince William County.

The bus started from Fairfax, went to Herndon, then on to Centerville and Manassas, said Payne, who took the same bus with his father.

"We started at 6 a.m., and we'd get there by 8 a.m. or 8:30 a.m.," he said. "It was a long, long ride. We left in the dark, and we came back in the dark."

Other black students who attended came from Baileys Crossroads, Vienna, Falls Church and Front Royal.

"It was a vocational school. They taught trades—welding, carpentry," he said. "It was strictly getting ready to begin a trade."

Before high school, Payne attended what was then called the "Fairfax Colored" elementary school—a wood-framed schoolhouse that once stood in front of the current Eleven Oaks school building at 10515 School St.

Recalling the years when he was a child and shortly afterward, Payne described the house he lived in as having no indoor plumbing. Outhouses served as bathrooms up until the 1970s, when sewers were finally installed in the neighborhood. A county spigot at the street corner was the only place to get fresh water, which in the winter was often problematic.

"If you didn't get it in the daytime, you went out in the morning and it was frozen," Payne said.

A house filled with seven children was sometimes chaotic, Payne said, but also fun.

"It was nice growing up. Everyone got along," he said. "You did your chores and learned to do them before dark."

During winter when the snow was heavy, there was no county snow removal service in Payne's neighborhood.

"Everyone had to chip in to shovel the snow. The whole neighborhood would chip in to clear the streets," he said.

Over winter and summer breaks, Payne and his mother, Virginia, worked on the farm, which was across from what is now the Country Club of Fairfax at 5110 Ox Road in Fairfax.

He said he and his siblings would pick blackberries when in season and his mother would make a sweet treat called blackberry mush.

"She was a good cook," Payne said, about his mother who died in 1981. "She was great at making cakes and pies."

About his father, Simon Atana Payne, he said he remembers him being a gentle man.

"It was a joy to have a mother and a father like I had," he said.[266]

"You do your part, and I will do mine."
—Jennie Dean

The founder of the Manassas Industrial School for Colored Youth was Jane Dean. Jane Serepta Dean (April 15, 1848–May 3, 1913), nicknamed Jennie or Miss Jennie, was born into slavery in northern Virginia and freed because of the American Civil War; she became an important founder of churches and Sunday schools for African Americans in northern Virginia. She was very active in the Northern Virginia Baptist Church Association. Dean founded this school in 1893, which existed for more than four decades. It was the only institution of secondary education available to African American youth in northern Virginia, including Prince William, Fairfax, Arlington, Loudoun and Fauquier Counties, for approximately two decades between 1938 until 1958.[267]

From 1870 to 1907, public education in Fairfax County was limited to an elementary education consisting of grades 1 through 7. However, from 1907 to 1954, there was no public high school in Fairfax County for African American children.

After World War II, there was a renewed push for an African American high school in Fairfax County. African American veterans met, with the full support of local Black churches, the Fairfax County Chapter of the NAACP and the Fairfax Countywide Colored Citizen Association. They organized to demand a high school for their children in Fairfax County. These meetings had hundreds of attendees and garnered much publicity. The churches were actively involved as meeting sites. These groups eventually had to threaten the school board and the Fairfax County school superintendent, Dr. Woodson, with a lawsuit in the early 1950s due to a lack of initiative on the county's part.[268] During this time, Atana Payne continued to take students back and forth to school in Manassas.

The McCandlish clan, as they like to call themselves, joined in as well. Mary Petersen, named after her mother, is mother to Virginia senator Chap Petersen. Mary's mother, Mary Walton (McCandlish) Livingston, joined the NAACP. She became a NAACP Person of the Year in 1951 in Fairfax County for her tireless efforts on behalf of equal rights under the law.[269]

During the 2023 Fairfax City Juneteenth celebration, Virginia state senator Chap Petersen spoke of a local civil rights crusader he knew in the School Street community. According to Petersen,

> *Stanley Smith lived on School Street for many, many years. He had been very active at city hall to help integrate all the Fairfax schools. His daughter, Carolyn Smith was the first black student that integrated into Lanier Middle School and then Fairfax High School. My grandmother tutored her once she began, to help catch her up from the courses she had not been taught. She always said, please let her in the front door. My great-aunt Nancy (McCandlish) Prichard had been her tutor during high school. I passed a House memorial resolution in 2004 about him. I met her at church in Vienna about a year ago. She remembered our family well.*[270]

> *The Legacy of an Archivist: Who Mary Walton Livingston Was Beyond Nixon's Tax Scandal*
> *By Jaya Patil,* Fairfax County Times
> *March 25, 2022*

> *Notorious for her part in denouncing then President Richard Nixon's 1969 income tax deduction claims amounting to nearly half a million dollars, Mary Walton Livingston's achievements tell part of the story of what a local legacy the civil rights activist and community leader was.*
> *Livingston was a Fairfax County native, born here in 1914. Her ancestral roots run deep in the county.*

Mary Walton McCandlish (*center, youngest*) in 1919; others unknown. The McCandlish family participated in bringing children from inner cities out to the county during the summer as part of the Fresh Air Initiative. *Photo courtesy of Tom Prichard.*

With no public high schools in Fairfax at the time, she graduated from National Cathedral School in Washington, D.C. and then Sweet Briar College in 1934.

After college, she returned and worked with the chamber, joining the National Archives and Records Administration (NARA) as an archivist, and became president of the Business and Professional Women's Club before the age of 25.

It was through the club that she met Schuyler William Livingston. They married in 1939 and built a house together, which she stayed in nearly all her life. While she stayed home with their three children, she was hard at work as a "leader in the community for civil rights," said her eldest daughter, Mary Petersen.

Before the Supreme Court's declaration for desegregation, Livingston led the first local interracial PTA and helped increase Black students' accessibility to schools—playing a part in the opening of James Lee Elementary. She was awarded a citation for her efforts by the Fairfax branch NAACP in 1951.

Following resistance to desegregation, Livingston worked on committees to keep public schools open and advocated for those discriminated against. "She was very cordial; she didn't just go and tell people what to do. She expressed it in the way she treated other people and wanted everyone to have opportunities," Petersen said.

In a 1961 letter to the mayor, after a baseball program advertised at an integrated school excluded a Black child on the grounds of segregation, Livingston requested that the Recreation Department's playground programs accommodate all children—expressing the disappointment of the situation for the child and alluding to the importance of equality "on a 'Big League' basis," as she put it.

"She enjoyed people so much, that's why she wanted everyone to have a chance to go to school, to participate in sports programs, and so on..."

Petersen said. "She knew and welcomed everybody." Her life and work spanned the transformation of Fairfax....

She was...a dedicated caretaker of her husband until he passed away from Alzheimer's in 1979. More than any awards or certificates, "She had such an influence on our family because of her commitment to her grandchildren and children," said Petersen. Livingston would take her grandchildren on Fridays, giving them memories of life and their parents some free time.

She spent her career as a senior archivist walking through 70,000 cubic feet of history and built as much in the community. Even after passing from Alzheimer's at 92, her impact continued with memorial contributions to her founding Immanuel Church-on-the-Hill or the Scholarship Fund of Alexandria.

Livingston's legacy lives on through her three children—Mary Peterson, Elizabeth Useem, and William Livingston—as well as 10 grandchildren and 11 great-grandchildren.[271]

Mrs. Livingston's brother-in-law, Edgar Prichard, also became involved. He had a more personal understanding despite his standing in the community. As an attorney, Prichard would go on to serve on the Fairfax Town/City Council from 1953 to 1964 and as mayor from 1964 to 1968. He successfully argued the "one man, one vote" case before the U.S. Supreme Court in 1962, which guaranteed full representation for Fairfax County in the general assembly.[272]

Tom Prichard, his son, said,

My father was raised in Montana. Until he was ten years old his family lived in a cabin, dirt floors, and no modern facilities in their home. He knew how hard life can be under these circumstances. The thing that saved him was his intelligence and studying hard in school. When he married his wife Nancy Montague McCandlish during World War II in Cairo, Egypt, both were working for the OSS, precursor to the CIA. They returned to live in her hometown of Fairfax at the conclusion of the war. He then earned a law degree and set up his practice in Fairfax, VA.[273]

In the fall of 1952, Edgar Prichard's law firm would expand from him and one brother-in-law to include both brothers-in-law. It would be called Livingston, McCandlish and Prichard. Their office was in the back room of the Moore house owned by Bam.[274]

Tom Prichard said,

> *Watching Atana's sacrifice and the pushback against a high school was very upsetting to him. My father decided he would have a visit with Dr. Woodson, the Superintendent of the Fairfax County Public Schools. He wanted him to understand that this was not just a one-sided issue. He was in full agreement with those wanting to file a lawsuit, including the very active Fairfax County Colored Citizen's Association. When he visited Superintendent Woodson, Prichard uncovered the reason why no school had been authorized. It was because it had to include water, sewer and plumbing to meet state code. Many had been denied such accommodations in their segregated neighborhoods. If they had it at school, Woodson surmised, they may demand it for their homes….My father looked him straight in the eye and said, "You were given state money to build a high school for African Americans. If you don't build it, I will sue you personally and the Fairfax County School District School Board myself."* [275]

The new high school broke ground soon thereafter, in 1953, without a lawsuit filed from either entity. Luther Porter Jackson High School opened in September 1954 as the high school for African American students in Fairfax County. Taylor M. Williams was the only principal of Luther

Downtown Fairfax in the 1950s. *Courtesy of Virginia Room, Fairfax County Public Library.*

Jackson High School and later served as Area 1 superintendent. In the landmark case *Brown vs. Board of Education*, on May 17, 1954, the Supreme Court issued a unanimous 9–0 decision in favor of the Browns. The court ruled that "separate educational facilities are inherently unequal," and therefore, laws that impose them violate the Equal Protection Clause of the Fourteenth Amendment of the U.S. Constitution.[276]

Luther Jackson High School marker.
Photo courtesy of Jenee Lindner.

Tom Prichard said, "Soon after the Supreme Court Ruling passed in 1954, the local chapter of the United Daughters of [the] Confederacy met at Mrs. McCandlish's home. This matriarch resigned on the spot and felt members were using their organization 'to vent their spleen against the Supreme Court.'"[277]

It would take another eleven years—until 1965—before Fairfax County Public Schools were integrated. The school was reopened as Luther Jackson Intermediate Middle School in September 1965, erasing by law segregation in the entire school district.

Several Jermantown Cemetery descendants said that besides educating, it was a community focal point, with the high school being a part of students', teachers' and parents' lives.

Chapter 4

DESEGREGATION IN FAIRFAX SCHOOLS AND THE RELOCATION OF GEORGE MASON UNIVERSITY

By Dr. Robert W. Prichard

The decision to move George Mason University from Bailey's Crossroads to the south side of Fairfax City in the 1960s was made at a time of heated debate in the Commonwealth of Virginia about the desegregation of what had been a segregated public school system.[278] While there were many motives for moving George Mason to the Fairfax campus, at least some of the advocates of the move supported relocation as an element in an effort to thwart plans for school desegregation.

Although the Supreme Court of the United States had ruled in 1954 that the segregation of public schools was unconstitutional, it took more than a decade for the decision to be implemented in many states. In the case of Virginia, the legislature actively opposed desegregation through a program of "massive resistance." No African American students were admitted to what had previously been all-White schools until after January 1959 decisions by federal courts and the Virginia Supreme Court to allow admission of selected students who petitioned the commonwealth for admission. In February 1959, four students entered Stratford Junior High School in Arlington. Norfolk schools admitted students that same month. Full integration of the schools took longer. In Arlington, it would not be until 1965 that Arlington closed the all-Black Hoffman-Boston Senior High School and not until 1971 that the school system adopted a bussing policy that integrated all schools in the country.[279] Other jurisdictions in the commonwealth lagged behind Arlington, with one county—Prince Edward—closing its schools until 1964 to prevent the admission of Black students.

The process was slower in Fairfax County than in Arlington and Norfolk, with the first African Americans entering selected schools in the 1960–61 school year. Three elementary schools, three intermediate schools and two high schools were affected. Of these schools, only one—Sydney Lanier Intermediate School—was in what was then the Town of Fairfax; Caroline Smith may have been the only African American student enrolled in Lanier that academic year.[280]

The mayor of the Town of Fairfax at the time, John C. Wood, and the majority of the city council had been supportive of segregated education and were unenthusiastic about ending it. The town of Fairfax had no schools of its own; however, the schools in the town were part of the Fairfax County school system. As a result, it would be county officials who made decisions about integration and school boundaries. Those in the town government who were opposed to desegregation reasoned that creating a separate school system of their own would give them more control over racial changes in the schools. They might, for example, refigure school boundaries. Much of the non-White population in the area straddled the southern border that divided the town from the county; one result of a separate school system might be ending Fairfax County's practice of sending some students from outside the boundary of the town of Fairfax to schools located in the town.

In order to create such a school system under Virginia law, however, Fairfax needed to become a city. The mayor and council sought status as a city, which was granted on July 1, 1961, soon after the end of the first academic year in which school desegregation began in Fairfax County. City officials then began the complicated process of withdrawing from the Fairfax County school system and of negotiating with the county to vacate its offices at the Fairfax Court House complex.

The departure of the county from the courthouse complex would leave a large hole in the center of the city and, conceivably, depress the local economy. Some supporters of a separate Fairfax City school system argued that relocating George Mason to the courthouse would mitigate the economic consequences of the departure of the county government.

As negotiations continued at a slow pace and the contours of the plan became clearer, one member of the city council, E.A. (Edgar Allen) Prichard (1920–2000), expressed his opposition. He ultimately resigned from the city council (on which he had served since 1953), announced his candidacy for mayor in the 1964 election and formed a "livable city slate" with a group of likeminded city residents to run against other council members. That Prichard took such a step was not surprising. Unlike most of the members of the city government, he was himself the product of an integrated school system: his first grade class had been one-third Native American.[281] In 1952, he had served as co-chair of an observance of National Brotherhood Week held at what was then known as the "James Lee Public School for Colored" in Falls Church.[282] He had also served as the attorney for the Colored Citizens' Protective League of Falls Church (which would become one of Virginia's first chapters of the NAACP) in its campaign for the construction of a modern high school for African Americans. That effort led to the opening of Luther Jackson High School in 1954.

In 1958, Prichard's activities attracted the attention of the "Thompson Committee," an investigative committee created by the Virginia legislature as part of its program of "massive resistance" to racial integration. The committee sought to identify and discredit supporters of school integration. Its 1958 interrogation of David Scull of Annandale included a specific question about E.A. Prichard's activities in support of school integration. Scull was jailed for his refusal to answer that and other questions, but he was exonerated the following year by the U.S. Supreme Court.[283]

If anything, the investigation of the Thompson Committee increased Prichard's support for civil rights. In August 1961, he came to the aid of the Mount Vernon Unitarian Church. The church had welcomed members of the Congress of Racial Equality (CORE) to its church buildings to conduct an eighteen-day "Virginia Action Institute," teaching "nonviolent methods of conducting sit-ins and other segregation protests." Fairfax County zoning administrator William T. Mooreland tried to stop the institute, alleging that teaching classes in a church in a residential neighborhood was in violation of county zoning ordinances; he threatened to evict the participants in the workshop and to arrest the church trustees. Prichard defended the action of the church and pointed out to the press and to the zoning authorities that the regulation that Mooreland cited included a provision allowing teaching in churches in residential neighborhoods.[284] Mooreland backed down, and the institute continued. Prichard also served without fee as the attorney for the extended family of William Clark, who owned a piece of property on Roberts Road, on the north side of Braddock. At a point in which many White attorneys were hesitant to assist Blacks desirous of home ownership, Prichard represented Clark in the subdivision of his property in order to give a portion of his land to his granddaughter Etta Bowles Richards (later Strozier) and her husband, Willis Richards, on which to build a home (1965). Prichard then represented the Richardses in subdividing their property so that their daughter Andrea and her husband, Robert Jones, could also build a home (1979).

In addition, E.A. Prichard's spouse, Nancy M. (McCandlish) Prichard, was known in the community for her opposition to segregation. In 1941, she had been the youngest member of the Virginia Electoral Reform League and the only female to testify against the poll tax at a hearing held by a Virginia legislative committee.[285] A former teacher, she assisted in the Head Start program for children living on School Street in Fairfax and tutored Caroline Smith in math after she entered Lanier Intermediate School.

E.A. Prichard and members of the slate won in elections in 1964 and again in 1966, overcoming a racist whisper campaign against them as "[N-word] lovers." The new mayor worked with the council to reverse the policy direction of the earlier administration. The city reached agreements with the County of Fairfax ceding jurisdiction of the courthouse complex (thereby allowing the county offices to remain in the city) and contracting with the county to provide instruction in the city schools. Prichard was reelected as mayor in 1966. It was during Prichard's time as mayor that the first African American staff member was hired to work for the city.

While Prichard disagreed with the previous mayor, Wood, on segregation, the two did agree on bringing George Mason College to the City of Fairfax. However, discussion shifted from the use of the courthouse for the school to center on a large tract of land owned by the Farr family. There was, however, one obstacle to moving to that site. The Farrs had given permission for Andy Smith, an African American who may have once worked for the family, to locate his trailer on a portion of that property fronting on Route 123. The permission was oral; no written contracts existed. The sale of the property to George Mason created a problem for Smith, since the Farr family did not offer an alternate location, and supporters of the new university were not anxious to have Smith's rather ramshackle trailer remain on university property.[286] The portion of the Farr land on which the trailer was located was in Fairfax County, which meant that the county's Health and Human Services Department arguably had the responsibility of assisting Mr. Smith. The department did not take a leading role in assisting Smith, however. With no one else offering a solution, Prichard suggested a way forward. Private donors offered funds to purchase a modern trailer for Smith, and the City of Fairfax offered a plot of land off of Pickett Road. Smith accepted the offer.

George Mason University moved to Fairfax City in August 1964, three months after the election of E.A. Prichard as mayor of the City of Fairfax. He was reelected in 1966 but chose not to run for a third term in 1968. He did, however, endorse Henry A. Minor as a candidate for one of the six seats on the city council to be filled that year. Minor, who ran fourth in a field of fifteen, became the first African American to serve on the council.[287]

After the end of his term as mayor, E.A. Prichard served the community in a variety of appointed and volunteer roles, including as a member of the board of trustees of George Mason University and as that body's rector (chair) from 1988 to 1991.

PART IV.

GEORGE MASON UNIVERSITY AND CENTER FOR MASON LEGACIES: BLACK LIVES NEXT DOOR

Left to right: Reverend Jeffery Johnson Sr., Mount Calvary Baptist Church in Fairfax, Virginia; Reverend Nelson Sneed, director and moderator of the Northern Virginia Baptist Association; and Dr. Gregory Washington, president of George Mason University. All spoke at the Juneteenth celebration in Fairfax, Virginia on June 17, 2023. *Photo courtesy of Jenee Lindner.*

Chapter 1

FREEDMEN OF NORTHERN VIRGINIA: INDEPENDENCE THROUGH LANDOWNERSHIP, BLACK COMMUNITIES AND THE NORTHERN VIRGINIA BAPTIST ASSOCIATION (EXCERPT)

By Marion Dobbins

As Reconstruction ended, freedmen in northern Virginia continued the process of community building through land acquisition. Contractual agreements deeding farmland from Whites to Blacks placed African Americans in a unique position of independence. Unlike sharecropping in the Deep South, proprietary rights in northern Virginia allowed autonomy in farming and financial stability to care for family and community. Additionally, Black property owners would philanthropically bestow sections of land to the community for religious and educational purposes, giving Blacks in Northern Virginia additional roads to prosperity. The ability to provide for the community's religious and educational needs was juxtaposed to those Blacks living in the lower South who were landless. In this region, through the establishment of organizations, a season of literacy, community responsibility and personal empowerment, along with financial and economic growth, was ushered in. In other words, landownership generated agency and self-determination by creating useful civic and religious organizations for freedmen in Northern Virginia.

Therefore, the Northern Virginia Baptist Association or NVBA was established to compliment the Black churches and address some of the social concerns. In his book *Under Their Own Vine and Fig Tree; The African-American Church in the South, 1865–1900*, William E. Montgomery maintains, "Blacks were striving to redefine their place in the economy. Their primary objective was the self-reliance their masters had denied them during slavery."[288] This denial included education, property ownership, control over their labor and, most of all, the inability to practice religion in the matter of their choosing. Most of the houses of worship in northern Virginia were organized by freedman (including Mount Calvary Baptist Church in Fairfax Court House) after the Civil War and provided duality in both religious and normal school teachings. It also afforded parishioners leadership roles in galvanizing their communities against the encroachment of inequality and Jim Crow.

Montgomery maintains, "District associations made their appearance almost as soon as independent black congregations were organized; some black associations actually antedated the Civil War."[289] Churches, along with religious associations, were important in forming a buffer against the severity of disenfranchisement. These religious institutions buttressed "the congregations as a political forum for discussing and acting on issues that affected the community…as practically the only black social institutions at the onset of freedom, churches provide[d] many services from education to recreation."[290] Black religious institutions, such as the Northern Virginia Baptist Association, provided those same types of services within the construct of this upper South region.

Indeed, as emancipation fostered independence for blacks in Northern Virginia, it also implemented a biracial free society, where Blacks and Whites attempted to create a postwar identity. However, in many instances, freedmen, wanting to become citizens, found opposition to this desire from native Whites in the area. According to historian Eric Foner, this era was not a seamless reconciliation; indeed, it was fraught with chaos, confusion and hardship. According to Foner, "All told, Reconstruction was the darkest page in the saga of American history."[291] Contrary to ex-slaves in the lower South, as the states transitioned from war to Reconstruction, the idea of land ownership began to become a reality in the minds of freed Blacks in northern Virginia. In simple terms, property helped Blacks gain equality with Whites. The ability to purchase land from northern White landowners provided economic stability and autonomy, thereby allowing Black farmers independence in crop growth and retail sales to large farmers markets in Washington, D.C. In McLean, dairy farmer Christopher Columbus Hall owned a multi-acre dairy and sold the milk at his own store in the District of Columbia.[292]

In Nan Netherton's book, *Fairfax County, Virginia: A History*, she argues, "Washington Markets allowed the community to thrive [and another example of this is] Cyrus Carter. Carter made an agreement to supply the Washington, D.C. jail with cabbage, string beans, corn, and other vegetables, while Christopher Columbus Hall, who came to Lincolnville from Loudoun County…established a 26-acre dairy farm in 1872."[293]

Another example of land ownership was Alfred Odrick in McLean. Living close to Lincolnville, after the Civil War, historical accounts state that Odrick was enslaved to the Coleman family, Robert G. and Ann Coleman of Dranesville, Virginia.[294] After emancipation, Odrick journeyed to Chicago and worked for a while as a carpenter. He later returned to the McLean area and, in 1872, acquired thirty acres of land in what is near the current-day Lewinsville Road. He purchased thirty acres of land for $450.[295] Odrick is also considered the founder of the "colored school" in the McLean, Lincolnville area. He donated a portion of his land for the erection of a schoolhouse to educate Black children.[296] Odrick, Carter and Hall all were early Black landowners who shaped an oasis of safety and security through their landownership. They were able to provide for their families through farming, commerce, religious participation and educational opportunities. These families created community through church organizing, school establishments and financial stability with their agrarian efforts.[297]

Held within the walls of the First Baptist Church of Warrenton, the organizational meeting of the Northern Virginia Baptist Association began in 1877.[298] The designated church, the Baptist church in Warrenton, had already been in existence since 1867 under the leadership of Reverend Waring. Reverend Waring and his charter members had purchased the property in 1867 on Lee Street in Warrenton for $400.[299] The one-hundred-year anniversary book claims that the founders were all ex-slaves still living within the Warrenton area when the congregation was formed. Historiography has shown that the organizing of religious societies directly after emancipation was not uncommon, and Fairfax County was no different. The NVBA provided small churches spread throughout the region to group together, forming a network of communication. This networking, listed in the 1891 minutes, included assistance with issues pertaining to morality, temperance, education, injustices and Christianity.[300] However, the question must be asked: How were these ex-slaves able to obtain $400 by 1867 to build a place of worship? Further research into this narrative needs to be done. From early minute books, research does show that the charter churches were within the borders of Fairfax, Prince William, Loudoun, Fauquier, Stafford, Page, Warren, Greene,

Rappahannock, Culpeper, Orange, Madison and a few in certain parts of West Virginia.[301]

An additional question is: Why was the organizational meeting selected at First Baptist of Warrenton? The answer is uncertain; however, one theory is that maybe Warrenton Baptist was one of the earliest established Black churches in Northern Virginia. In the 1891 annual meeting minutes, it boasted more members than any other church in the area.[302] Furthermore, the Blacks living within the Prince William County and Warrenton County borders were in proximity to each other and were organizing a vocational school for colored youth. This school, Manassas Industrial School for Colored Youth, was the brainchild of Miss Jennie Dean, who had been enslaved on the Cushing Plantation near the current-day Manassas Battlefield.[303] Dean is listed in the 1891 minutes for the convention held at Pleasant Grove in Orange County as a leader for the Sunday School Union and the Moral and Temperance Committee.

Because Dean was involved in organizing the "colored" secondary school and First Baptist Warrenton had the largest membership of any church, this may be the reason for the first conference being held outside of Fairfax County. Furthermore, the original moderator of the Association was Reverend Marshall D. Williams DD, the minister at the time for First Baptist of Warrenton.[304] Looking at ministers who organized churches in Fairfax County, such as Cyrus Carter, none had an educational background or a Doctor of Divinity degree.

In July 1889, a group of twenty-one churches met in Culpeper at the Antioch Baptist Church.[305] A resolution was drafted to organize an additional association in the region, as the breadth of churches within NVBA was large. The main reason for division was mobility and transportation issues for such a large organization, spreading from Washington, D.C., to West Virginia. This resolution was passed, and another group, the New Wayland Blue Ridge Association, was created and served the churches in and around the Culpeper area. However, the Northern Virginia Baptist Association would continue to serve the churches within Fairfax, such as First Baptist Church of Merrifield, Second Baptist of Falls Church and Shiloh, as well as Mount Calvary Baptist Church of Fairfax.[306]

An overview of responsibilities listed within the initial constitutional bylaws to which the NVBA adheres contains the following: "Objects of this Association shall be for fraternal intercourse and mutual counsel: to promote the union of churches: to promote Christian and general education: to advance the cause of Christ by all means consistent with the Word of

God."[307] Added goals within the Baptist Association were to assist the community churches in sustaining themselves financially and creating new religious facilities in the area.[308] The associations such as the NVBA gave congregations and especially Black males an opportunity to gather together and voice their opinions on current-day topics and provided support for new churches, schools and missionaries.[309]

Chapter 2

THE IMMIGRANT:
JOHN MORARITY (A.K.A. MORIARTY)

By Anne Dobberteen

John Morarity (a.k.a. Moriarty) was an Irish immigrant who purchased land from Judge Henry Thomas. This land became an anchor for the Black community: his land would eventually house descendants and extended family, baseball diamonds and much of the Eleven Oaks Elementary School campus.

Morarity was born around 1831 and probably came to the United States as a young man, arriving in Fairfax by the 1850s. It is possible that he accompanied Irish people sailing across the ocean to American mid-Atlantic ports. These immigrants answered labor-recruiting advertisements placed by the Orange & Alexandria Railroad Company to work on a railroad line passing through Providence (renamed Fairfax in 1874). A biographical sketch available at the Fairfax County Historic Records Center states that Morarity took the oath of U.S. citizenship in 1859 and voted at the Fairfax Court House that year.[310] During the Civil War, he worked on the Allison family plantation called Hibernia, a tract that is now part of the George Mason University campus facing Chain Bridge Road. There is no evidence that Morarity joined the military or saw combat. After the defeat of the Confederacy, he sued the Allisons for back wages. In 1879 legal testimony, he confirmed his employment with Robert Allison, a farmer. The illiterate Morarity signed a court document with the mark *X*.[311]

Morarity had a long-term romantic relationship with an African American woman named Eliza Turley. It is unlikely that the two were legally married, but they lived together, and the couple created a family together when White and Black people were discouraged from doing so. Eliza may have been enslaved by the Allisons, and it is likely that she and John Morarity became intimate at Hibernia; more research is needed on her possible enslavement. Eliza Turley and John Morarity had their first child, Joseph (Tobe), shortly before the Civil War. Sources present different birth dates for Joseph, ranging from ca. 1857 to ca. 1860. Five more children followed: George, Sina, John R., Daniel and Thomas.[312]

After weathering the Civil War and navigating Reconstruction, Eliza Turley succumbed to complications as she was birthing a newborn at Hibernia in 1874; her infant son also perished. That she passed away on the Allison property indicated that she had retained a tie to a place where she may have once been held in bondage.

Dorcas Pearson and John Morarity each reported the demise of Eliza Turley and her infant son. Dorcas was Eliza's female acquaintance, whose knowledge of the deceased baby's sex suggests proximity to Turley's fatal delivery. Dorcas reported that Eliza's sister-in-law Amy Turley also perished in childbirth that year. Most important, Dorcas named her late friend Eliza *Morarity*, thereby identifying her as the wife of John Morarity. But John, likely the deceased baby's father, called his partner Eliza *Turley*; there was no reference to a spousal relationship. The Fairfax *Register of Deaths* suggests that John had initially self-identified as Eliza's husband, but he evidently decided not to disclose this detail after her passing. The *Register of Deaths* entry shows that the recorder started to enter "John" in the "Consort of, or Unmarried" column but then simply listed Eliza as unmarried. Toward the end of Reconstruction, the widower may have chosen to dissociate himself from his late partner, perhaps fearing that the courthouse official handling the register might cause trouble for the Morarity family. It could have been the case that the couple were also separated or estranged when Eliza and her infant died.[313]

Nevertheless, John did not remove himself from Fairfax's Black community, nor did he disown his children with Eliza. The 1880 U.S. Census placed John, his sons and his daughter in Jermantown—i.e., the "colored" part of town—with Robert Hunter's household in "Dwelling 413." During the next decade, Morarity entered a rent-to-purchase contract for ten acres of land belonging to Judge Henry Thomas. Hunter, the "mulatto" man whom the Moraritys knew well, entered into a similar agreement to purchase another parcel of Thomas property in 1883 facing Chain Bridge Road.[314] The 1902–1903 Fairfax County Voter Registers list John Morarity as White but indicate he was associated with the Black community with a "col" notation by his name. If we assume that he had moved to the land he had bought from Thomas by that time, next to Hunter's, this would indicate that the area on and around Thomas's property was becoming home to at least some of Fairfax's Black community by that point.[315]

Generations of Moraritys lived in Fairfax on or near a parcel of land. John Morarity's son Thomas's 1890 marriage certificate, recording his union with Luvenia "Venie" Gibson, stated that John and Eliza Morarity were the groom's married parents. This document clearly indicates that the family patriarch and matriarch were remembered by one of their children as husband and wife. All of John and Eliza's children were identified as "colored" or "mulatto" in census and marriage documents, indicating that their community ties were with the African Americans of Fairfax; they were not persons who used a light skin color to "pass" into White society, leaving their families and roots behind.[316] These Morarity descendants became pillars of Fairfax's Black community; one grandson, Warren "Chick" Morarity, opened a popular convenience store across the street from his family's property in 1948.[317] Another grandson, Lewis Morarity, was a leader of the Mt. Calvary Baptist Church.

In his last will and testament, John Morarity legally recognized the sons and daughter he had with Eliza. The will made provisions for his children to inherit sections of the ten acres he bought from Judge Thomas in 1890.[318] Two Morarity sons were not listed in his will; these children, George and Thomas, had already established themselves as owners of parcels of the original ten acres. In 1951, the Morarity descendants still held title to the land that they inherited, although some had not built on it. The next year, Robert D. Graham acquired this undeveloped Morarity property on behalf of the Fairfax School Board to expand the Rosenwald School into a new Eleven Oaks Elementary campus for segregated public use and the education of Black children in 1952.[319]

John Morarity could not have known that his property would become an institutional center of Fairfax's Black community. When he succumbed to cancer in 1904, whoever was responsible for his obituary in the local town paper chose to remember his work as a janitor for the clerk of the court; there was no mention in this death notice of surviving Morarity family members.[320]

It is not difficult to imagine John Morarity, a poor Irishman likely facing anti-immigrant prejudice in a new country, experiencing significant challenges in Virginia. He nevertheless found employment and managed to save money to purchase ten acres of land for his descendants near the end of his life. He and his partner, or wife, Eliza, navigated the Civil War and Reconstruction as the patriarch and matriarch of a working class, mixed-race family who eventually enjoyed the security of home ownership on that land that would come to be known as School Street.[321]

Chapter 3

THE SEGREGATIONIST DAIRY FARMER:

JOHN S. BARBOUR

By Anne Dobberteen

John Strode Barbour (1866–1952) was a prominent White lawyer and dairy farmer who bought Henry Thomas's land from the judge's heirs.[322] In the 1910s and 1920s, Barbour sold parcels of his property, abutting the family land of Robert Hunter and John Morarity, to members of Fairfax's Black community; these transactions included plots on which the Rosenwald School and Mt. Calvary Baptist Church were built. In so doing, Barbour provided opportunities for Black homeownership, education and collective worship in racially segregated Fairfax City.

Born in August 1866, Barbour came from an old Virginia family that owned the "Beauregard" estate in Culpepper. He earned a degree from the University of Virginia and practiced law as a recent graduate in his hometown before moving his offices to Fairfax in 1907. Through the legal profession, he engaged in business, civic and political affairs, serving as counsel for the Washington Railway and Electric Company and Potomac Electric Power Company; he was a member of the State Library Board and one of the founders of the Fairfax Town Library Association; and he also belonged to the Fairfax Rotary Club, Sons of the Confederate Veterans and the Maryland and Virginia Milk Producers Association.[323] In 1902, he participated in the Virginia Constitutional Convention that codified Jim Crow–era restrictions (voting, residential, economic and social) imposed on Black and poor White people in Virginia. Barbour was part of a broader moment of backlash led by conservative Democrats against gains made by African Americans during the Reconstruction period following the Civil War.[324]

Barbour's real estate transactions in Fairfax City reinforced de jure segregation in the town, but he opened up lots in his subdivision for Black families to own homes and build wealth. The presence of the Moraritys and Robert Hunter likely encouraged him on this path. Seeing that the border of his dairy farm was already home to some Black families, Barbour could have decided to subdivide the acres near it for Black buyers as a practical business move. Thanks to its bovine inhabitants, the area may have had an odor at times that could have caused White families looking to buy to go elsewhere, leaving Barbour with only African American buyers who may have had fewer choices.

Barbour helped cluster the Black community on the south side of East School Street. He sold two (nearly) half-acre lots to an African American buyer named Henson Turner in 1912 and 1913.[325] Robert Newton bought one of Turner's lots in 1916 for $150.[326] Barbour sold a lot to Emma Lucas next to one of Turner's lots in 1917.[327] In 1920, Barbour sold about one acre to Lucy Naylor, who was required to build a "substantial woven wire fence around" her property, "separating it from the residue of said Barbour's land sufficient to protect the same against trespass from horses, cattle, sheep, hogs, and chickens."[328] That same year, Barbour sold a lot to Georgia Chambers with the same fence stipulation.[329] Then, in 1921, he sold a narrow lot next to the Lucas property to Stephen and Mabel Payne.[330]

Barbour also made it possible for the Rosenwald School and Mt. Calvary Baptist Church, two Black-run institutions, to relocate to the "colored" section of Fairfax City neighboring his property. He contracted to sell two lots of his subdivision to the Fairfax Colored School League to build the school in 1917 for $500. This new school meant that the old Fairfax Colored School, located close to the Court House and thereby more spatially integrated into the professional center of town, would no longer draw Black students through that area every day. Instead, Black pupils would be drawn to what was rapidly becoming a Black neighborhood for their education. In this instance of municipal social engineering, the discriminatory "separate but equal" concept, enshrined into law by the *Plessy v. Ferguson* Supreme Court decision (1896), underpinned these maneuvers.[331]

Decades later, in 1949, Barbour and his wife finalized the terms of another sale of land to the trustees of the African American Mt. Calvary Baptist Church, currently situated on the north side of School Street. This transaction enabled Mt. Calvary Baptist worshippers to move their services to a bigger modern building in 1957; the previous church location a few blocks north of Chain Bridge Road and Armstrong Street could no longer accommodate the congregation. The asking price, $1,200, was made payable in four installments over four years at a 5 percent interest rate. The down payment was $240. Among the Mt. Calvary Baptist trustees was Lewis Morarity, a grandson of both John Morarity and Strother Gibson, who had been a church founder in 1870. Lewis Morarity belonged to a group of religious leaders that included Ernest Pinn, James Hunter, Marvin Metcalf, Atana Payne and John Martin. The siting of Mt. Calvary Baptist in the School Street area represented another southward shift of a Black institution away from the center of Fairfax City.[332]

Although a segregationist, Barbour supported the growth of School Street neighborhood infrastructure. This fact highlights that twentieth-century residential developments in Fairfax did not always follow a predictable or uniformly determined script.[333] There may yet be a 1930s New Deal–era redlining history to uncover, which doomed Black homeowners to low property values and unequal access to housing loans, but we have found no evidence of this in Barbour's dealings.[334] What we now know is that Barbour seemed to be operating as a real estate agent in a field that he defined according to his personal aims: that of making money from willing buyers on transactional terms that were favorable to him and, in the process, concentrating a Black community and its infrastructure to a racially segregated area of Fairfax City farther from the town center.[335]

Chapter 4

FAMILY CONNECTIONS: MATRILINEAL ROOTS OF THE SCHOOL STREET COMMUNITY

By Anne Dobberteen

A close examination of matrilineal lines of descent reveals the deep connections of Black School Street residents to each other and the land. The Gibson and Morarity families are a case in point. Two sisters, Luvenia "Venie" and Martha Gibson, took their husbands' last names and stayed for decades in this area of Fairfax City. Venie and Martha were the daughters of Strother (1846–1927) and Martha Gibson (1844–1926), a prominent married couple in the Black community. Martha had been enslaved prior to the Civil War somewhere in Virginia; Strother was likely enslaved as a child before his father, Horace Gibson, purchased his own and his family's freedom from the portion of his earnings as a blacksmith that he was allowed by his White master to keep.

Horace Gibson owned a successful blacksmithing business in Fairfax County. He was based in an area near Fairfax City then called Ilda. In 1884, Strother bought fourteen acres alongside Braddock Road from Albert Dewey. On this purchased tract, Strother erected a log cabin home for his large family of thirteen children. Venie and Martha Gibson grew up in this household. Strother was a founding member of the Mt. Calvary Baptist Church and active in the state Republican party; he was elected in April 1892 as a Fairfax delegate to the Congressional Convention. He also worked for the Willard family (of the Willard Hotel in Washington, D.C.) for many years, starting his employment as a teenager. He became the personal attendant to Colonel Joseph Willard during the Civil War before moving to a maintenance and service job on the Willard property in Fairfax. When he died in 1927, Strother's probated estate included a horse, buggy, personal affects and $536.78 in the National Bank of Fairfax, equivalent to $8,673.25 in 2022 dollars.[336]

In 1896, Luvinia (alternatively spelled Lavinia, Louvenia or Venie) Gibson married Thomas Morarity, John Morarity's son. Seven years later, she bought a parcel of land from her father-in-law and thereafter lived on this smallholding. Luvenia was active in Mt. Calvary Baptist and organized community fundraising dinners that courted wealthy White Fairfax doctors and lawyers to donate to her church. Venie Gibson Morarity died in 1949. Surviving relatives included her daughter Mabel (Payne) and sons Victor, Warren, Lewis and Lloyd Morarity.[337]

Venie and Thomas's children stayed geographically close to their family home. In 1930, Warren and his wife, Evelyn L. Morarity, bought land across the street in the Rust subdivision once owned by Frederick Murray. This property bordered Route 123. In 1948, Warren and Evelyn opened a variety store on an adjacent lot, identified as lot 41 in the 1962 tax map.[338] Mabel Morarity Payne and her husband, Stephen Payne, purchased a property a few steps away from her parents' home in the Barbour subdivision in 1921 and later subdivided this parcel for Mabel's brother Lewis Morarity and his wife, Beatrice.[339] Mabel's daughter Dorothy Payne and her spouse, Lester Page, built a home on the Morarity land as well.[340] Lewis Morarity was a clerk at Mt. Calvary Baptist for twenty-plus years. Lester Page operated a plumbing business with customers in Washington, D.C.[341]

Martha Gibson Groomes, Venie's sister, held title to her own land in the School Street area. She lived diagonally across from Venie on Route 123.[342] Martha married Bradshaw "Brad" Groomes in 1910 in Washington, D.C., and they had three children: Gilbert, Virginia and Dorothy. Brad Groomes had a variety of jobs. He hosted picnics and music concerts in nearby Greenwood Park.[343] He also raised hogs, collected and sold scrap metal and was caught selling alcohol illegally more than once. Martha was employed as a housecleaner. The couple divorced in 1943. That year, Brad Groomes bought a lot in the East School Street neighborhood from his brother, B.A. Groomes, next to Luvenia Morarity's plot. B.A. Groomes had purchased his land from one of the Moraritys. Brad died in 1947 and does not seem to have moved out of Martha's home onto his new plot; Martha followed him to the grave in 1949.[344]

The land Brad Groomes bought from his brother B.A. Groomes passed to Bradshaw and Martha's daughter, Virginia Williams, after Brad's death. This chain of ownership and transferring of title demonstrates how pioneering Black families in the School Street area held onto the land as a source of wealth for multiple generations. Virginia Williams eventually sold the parcel that she inherited from her father to the Fairfax County Redevelopment Authority in 1991 for $440,000.[345] Interviewed by the *Washington Post* about the property transaction, Virginia Williams elaborated on pivotal moments and processes shaping Black history around Chain Bridge Road. She lived in a separate home on a different lot on the other side of School Street at the time.[346]

These short stories of the Gibsons, the Groomes and the Moraritys, and the White men whom they bought or inherited land from, are just one tiny part of how one of Black Fairfax's communities became established as property and homeowners during the late nineteenth and early twentieth centuries. More remains to be discovered about other School Street families and other Black families in the greater Fairfax City area. Using property records, newspapers and census records, we hope to broaden our scope and continue to tell a richer story about Black homeownership, community and intergenerational wealth in Fairfax.[347]

PART V.

THE FUTURE

Titus Prescott, a rising senior at Centreville High School, has many ancestors in the Jermantown Cemetery. *Photo courtesy of Rondia Prescott, his mother.*

Chapter 1

JERMANTOWN CEMETERY
PRESERVATION SOCIETY

By Etta Willson, Rita Colbert, Linneall Naylor, Rondia Prescott and Jenee Lindner

Jermantown Cemetery Preservation Society mission statement is: "To identify, document, preserve, protect, maintain, and advocate for the Jermantown Cemetery."

1. Focus on the appearance of the cemetery
2. Get a surveyor to locate the exact boundaries of the cemetery
3. Put a fence around the cemetery to protect it
4. Landscape the cemetery to make it look more serene and peaceful
5. Focus on signage and a historical marker for the cemetery

Cemetery descendants celebrate Jermantown Cemetery Legacy Day, August 2023, at Mount Calvary Baptist Church, Fairfax, Virginia. *Photo courtesy of Linneall Naylor.*

Cemetery descendants and church hosts celebrate the first Jermantown Cemetery Legacy Day, August 2022, at Truro Anglican Church, Fairfax, Virginia. *Left to right*: Tony Zipfel, Ron Crittendon, Rondia Prescott, Dayna "Sam" Burns, Rita Colbert, Virginia Payne, Etta Allen Willson, Sue Colbert, Jenee Lindner, Linneall Naylor, Jeremiah Murphy, Angela Payne, Connie Smith (*back*), Evelyn Grant (*front*), Earl Marshall (*back*), Vera Wilkes (*back*), Alcie Metcalf (*front*), Dr. Edward Jones (*back*), Linda Coates Anderson (*front*), Robert MacKay (*back*), Catherine Jefferson Kirkley. *Photo courtesy of Jenee Lindner.*

6. Place grave markers in the cemetery to validate all who are buried there
7. Focus on discovering all who are buried in the cemetery.
8. Place a StoryMap online and in the cemetery for visitors to know who is buried there
9. Get the cemetery deemed a historical landmark

Globally, 25 percent trace their homeland to China, 23 percent to India, 17 percent to parts of Asia and the Pacific, 18 percent to Europe, 10 percent to Africa and 7 percent to the Americas.[348] We are one large family.

We will continue looking for African Americans buried here or who lived here in the Fairfax, Virginia area. We will continue to search our collective family trees. There is an old saying: "Nobody really dies until they are forgotten." We will not forget. We shall find them all by name.

NOTES

INTRODUCTION

1. Virginia census records, Ancestry.com.
2. "City History," City of Fairfax Virginia, https://www.fairfaxva.gov/government/historic-resources/city-history.
3. Virginia census records, Ancestry.com.
4. Andrew M.D. Wolf, *Black Settlement in Fairfax County, Virginia During Reconstruction* (Fairfax County, VA: Fairfax County Office of Comprehensive Planning, 1975), 63.
5. Virginia census records, Ancestry.com.
6. U.S. Census records.
7. Fairfax County Office of Research and Statistics Management Services Branch, *Fairfax County 1981 Profile*, 2–11.
8. U.S. Department of Defense, "75 Years of the GI Bill: How Transformative It's Been," January 9, 2019, https://www.defense.gov/News/Feature-Stories/story/Article/1727086/75-years-of-the-gi-bill-how-transformative-its-been/.
9. Smithsonian Art Museum, "After the War: Blacks and the G.I. Bill," https://americanexperience.si.edu/wp-content/uploads/2015/02/After-the-War-Blacks-and-the-GI-Bill.pdf.
10. World Population Review, "Fairfax County, Virginia Population 2023," https://worldpopulationreview.com/us-counties/va/fairfax-county-population.

Part I

Chapter 1

11. "On December 31, 1866, the trustees of the Ladies Memorial Association paid Richard T. Brown and his wife, Marion, $225.00 for 2⅓ acres…[it was for Whites only].The Ladies Memorial Association did not last long as a viable organization, and in March of 1875 ownership of the cemetery was conveyed to the trustees of the newly chartered Fairfax Cemetery Association.…The Fairfax Cemetery Association acquired additional property in 1914 and 1932. Control of the cemetery was passed to the newly incorporated City of Fairfax in 1962." Excerpts from Brian A. Conley, *Cemeteries of Fairfax County, Virginia* (Fairfax County, VA: Fairfax County Public Libraries, 1994).

12. Walter Pierce Park Cemeteries, "The Benevolent Association, 1838–1923," https://walterpierceparkcemeteries.org/the-free-young-mens-colored-union-benevolent-association/.

13. *Fairfax News*, May 30, 1873.

14. "The Benevolent Association, 1838–1923."

15. Ibid.

16. Ibid.

17. "History of the Clerk's Office," Official Site of Fairfax County, https://www.fairfaxcounty.gov/circuit/historic-records-center/clerks-office-history.

18. Nan Netherton et al., *Fairfax, Virginia: A City Traveling Through Time* (Fairfax, VA: History of the City of Fairfax Round Table, 1997), 11.

19. Ibid., 35.

20. 1865 Freedmen's Bureau Census, Fairfax County, Virginia; *Alexandria Gazette*, November 21, 1865.

21. Special Order No. 9, James I Ferree, Sept. 4, 1865. "Virginia, Freedmen's Bureau Field Office Records, 1865–1872," FamilySearch, https://familysearch.org/pal:/MM9.3.1/TH-267-11767- 180107-25?cc=1596147.

22. J.W. Bushong to Sidney B. Smith, October 10, 1865. "Virginia, Freedmen's Bureau Field Office Records, 1865–1872," FamilySearch, https://familysearch.org/pal:/MM9.3.1/TH-267-11600- 111191-24?cc=1596147.

23. National Archives, Washington D.C.; Freedman's Bureau Records: Fairfax Courthouse and County; Roll 75: November 29, 1865.

24. Hareem Badil-Abish, *Shades of Gray: A Beginning—The Origins and Development of a Black Family in Fairfax, Virginia*, edited by Dennis Howard (self-published, 2006; available at the Fairfax County Public Library), 18–19.

25. Edward Coleman Trexler Jr., *Early African Americans, Families of Fairfax Courthouse, Virginia, Origins* (James River Valley, 2012), 24.

26. Patricia Hickin, in Nan Netherton, et al., *Fairfax County, Virginia: A History* (1978), 379.

27. Fairfax County Deed Book (hereafter DB) 1–4, p. 429–30.

28. Trexler, *Early African Americans*, 36–38.

29. Fairfax County DB 1–4, p. 429–30.

30. Fairfax County DB 1–4, p. 231, Fairfax County Circuit Court Historic Records Center (hereafter FCCHRC).

31. Trexler, *Early African Americans*, 34.

32. Fairfax Minute Book 1880, p. 188 (submitted November 17, 1887), letter to Judge James Keith re: Jermantown Cemetery, p. 1, FCCHRC.

33. Library of Virginia; Richmond, Virginia; Virginia, U.S., Death Registers, 1853–1911, p. 135; browse level: 62152_I870349.

34. "Alfred Whaley," Find a Grave, https://www.findagrave.com/memorial/68876272/alfred-whaley.

35. *Fairfax Times* or *Fairfax Herald*, n.d.

36. 1870 United States Federal Census; Year: 1870; Census Place: Providence, Fairfax, Virginia; Roll: M593_1645; Page: 366A.

37. Fairfax County Circuit Court Historic Resources: Fairfax County DB: J4, p. 331.

38. Year: 1880; Census Place: Providence, Fairfax, Virginia; Roll: 1364; Page: 364C; Enumeration District: 038.

39. Ibid.

40. Trexler, *Early African Americans*, 23.

41. Debbie Robison, "Little River Turnpike Constructed 1802–11," Northern Virginia History Notes, September 20, 2017, http://www.novahistory.org/LittleRiverTurnpike/LittleRiverTurnpike.htm.

42. Fairfax DB: C5, p. 255, FCCHRC; Vincent D. Sutphin; *Nothing Remains the Same: Jermantown, Legato, Pender, and Waples Mill During the 1920s and 1930s in Fairfax County, Virginia* (Fairfax, VA: History4All, 2009), 18.

43. Year: 1880; Census Place: Providence, Fairfax, Virginia; Roll: 1364; Page: 345B; Enumeration District: 038.

44. Year:1870; Census Place: Providence, Fairfax, Virginia, Roll: M593_1645; Page: 368A.

45. Year: 1880; Census Place: Providence, Fairfax, Virginia; Roll: 1364; Page: 345B; Enumeration District: 038.
46. Sutphin, *Nothing Remains the Same*, 38.
47. Ancestry.com, U.S. Find a Grave Index, 1600—Current.
48. Ibid.
49. "The Educators of Dranesville District," Fairfax County Public Schools, https://www.fcps.edu/about-fcps/history/records/dranesville/biographies.
50. Ibid.
51. Ibid.
52. Library of Virginia; Richmond, Virginia; Virginia, U.S., Death Registers, 1853–1911, p. 135; browse level: 62152_I870349.
53. "Braddock District Black History Month," Official Site of Fairfax County, https://www.fairfaxcounty.gov/braddock/braddock-district-black-history-month?fbclid=IwAR3YGlSzw26aHkKa2LuDHNedr5x3uLe30J8IbzvSYPbR0tIXetSF3ewsNPs.
54. Virginia Department of Health; Richmond, Virginia; Virginia Deaths, 1912–2014; 1927 Death Certificate: 24256-24840; p. 80.
55. Book 1880, p. 188 (submitted November 17, 1887), Letter to Judge James Keith re: Jermantown Cemetery, p. 1, FCCHRC.
56. Fairfax City Walking Tour notes from author.
57. Ibid.
58. Letter to Judge James Keith re: Jermantown Cemetery, p. 1.
59. Badil-Abish, *Shades of Gray*, 34–38.
60. Ibid., 40-42.
61. Virginia Department of Health; Richmond, Virginia; Virginia Deaths, 1912–2014, Ancestry.com.
62. Virginia, U.S., Select Marriages, 1785–1940; Ancestry.com.
63. Letter to Judge James Keith re: Jermantown Cemetery, 1.
64. Virginia, U.S., Select Marriages, 1785–1940; Ancestry.com, FHL Film Number: 31329; Reference ID: 69-35.
65. "The Benevolent Association, 1838–1923."
66. Fairfax Minute Book 14, p. 116, FCCHRC.
67. Donald Sweig, ed., *Registrations of Free Negroes Commencing September Court 1822, Book Number 2* and *Register of Free Blacks 1835 Book 3, Being the Full Text of the Two Extent Volumes 1822 through 1861, of Registrations of Free Blacks Now in the County Courthouse, Fairfax, Virginia* (Fairfax, VA: Fairfax County Office of Comprehensive Planning, July 1977). George Lamb: Register No. 450, p. 218.

68. William Page Johnson II, *Cousins and Brothers* (Fairfax, VA: Iberian, 1995); Ron Baumgarten, "All Not So Quiet Along the Potomac: The Civil War in Northern Virginia & Beyond," March 31, 2011.
69. Seventeenth Virginia, Company D "Fairfax Rifles," https://www.fairfax-rifles.org.
70. Obituary published in the *Fairfax Herald*, March 26, 1926. Special thanks to Andrea Loewenwarter for sharing her research.
71. "Corp Maurice Watson Harris," Find a Grave, https://www.findagrave.com/memorial/8494777/maurice-watson-harris.
72. Discussion with author during a Jermantown Cemetery reorganization meeting at Mount Calvary Baptist Church, September 2021.

Chapter 2

73. "Jermantown Cemetery," Find a Grave, https://www.findagrave.com/cemetery/1979740/jermantown-cemetery.
74. Michael Laris, "Fairfax Moves Forward with Cemetery for the Poor," *Washington Post*, June 23, 2013, https://www.washingtonpost.com/local/trafficandcommuting/fairfax-moves-forward-with-cemetery-for-the-poor/2013/06/23/fa08cf2a-d378-11e2-a73e-826d299ff459_story.html.
75. January 21, 2022 email exchange between Karen Teresa Hannigan and author: "11085 Fairfax Blvd. is the location of the [Jermantown] cemetery you were asking about, definitely no county involvement at this site."
76. Fairfax County Circuit Court, Fairfax, VA; Trustee Case: Jermantown Cemetery # 2014—13018.
77. Ibid.
78. Virginia nonprofits: notes found on Jermantown Cemetery Grave Preservation Society nonprofit 501(c)3, 2015–2018, https://cis.scc.virginia.gov/.
79. Ibid.
80. "In Humility to Listen, Learn and Serve." In the fall of 2019, a Fairfax, Virginia group later called the racial unity reconciliation group (RRG) made up of faith-based, grassroots community members focused on building relationships with individuals, churches and organizations for racial healing and justice. In June 2020, they took a multi-week course developed by Coracle Interfaith Racial Unity Group at https://inthecoracle.org/. Historical lessons and Laments were studied. This course became the core foundation for their work. The RRG later

expanded to all of Fairfax County and beyond. Many others took the course. It now has a diverse, two-hundred-person membership. RRG mission areas of prayer, education, service and policy guide their efforts. They have met by Zoom weekly to listen to each other in humility, build understanding, lift each other and act to make positive change through service and policy. Their desire is to see and love each other, perform actionable service, and through transformative relationships, bring healing and reconciliation in accordance with the Lord's calling. Scripture motto: "He has shown you, O mortal, what is good. And what does the Lord require of you? To act justly and to love mercy and to walk humbly with your God." —*Micah 6:8 (NIV)*

81. Will Rowe, "Preservation Plan for Jermantown Cemetery."

82. Virginia nonprofits: notes found on Jermantown Cemetery Grave Preservation Society nonprofit 501(c)3, 2015–2018, https://cis.scc.virginia.gov/.

83. Heather Zwicker, "People and Places—Week of November 26, 2021: Volunteers Clean Up Historic Jermantown Cemetery," *Fairfax County Times*, https://www.fairfaxtimes.com/articles/people_and_places/people-and-places---week-of-november-26-2021/article_92fab312-4c81-11ec-be22-030e4f68db18.html.

84. Jaya Patil, "Fairfax Woman Forms Nonprofit to Preserve Jermantown Cemetery," *Fairfax County Times*, March 18, 2022, updated March 23, 2022, https://www.fairfaxtimes.com/articles/fairfax_county/fairfax-woman-forms-nonprofit-to-preserve-jermantown-cemetery/article_28d7faee-a61d-11ec-b91c-4704e183fda8.html?msclkid=71d836ddcf1111eca4f11775e124b6c2.

85. Linneall Naylor, official Fairfax County Circuit Court documents.

86. Author notes from History Fairfax City Inc. Fairfax City Walking Tour Manual.

87. Trexler, *Early African Americans*, 36, 86–87.

88. Fairfax County Circuit Court Historic Resources: Fairfax County DB 1–4, p. 231.

Chapter 3

89. "Senator Petersen Feb. 28th Black History Month Senate Floor Speech," Raphaël Debraine, YouTube video, posted May 10, 2022, www.youtube.com/watch?v=q8wREGTpXBU.

90. From *This Was Virginia 1900–1927 as Shown by Glass Negatives of J. Harry Shannon, the Rambler*, compiled by Connie and Mayo Stuntz, courtesy of Fairfax County Public Library.
91. Michael Marrow, "Family's History in Vienna Spans 160+ Years." *Fairfax County Times*, February 25, 2022, updated March 7, 2022, https://www.fairfaxtimes.com/articles/fairfax_county/family-s-history-in-vienna-spans-160-years/article_c3671608-95ab-11ec-8fe5-effb54c04133.html.
92. Badil-Abish, *Shades of Gray*.
93. Kate B. Carter, ed., "Mississippi Saints," in *Our Pioneer Heritage* (Salt Lake City: Daughters of Utah Pioneers, 1958), 421–76; William E. Parrish, "The Mississippi Saints," *Historian* 50, no. 4 (August 1988): 489–506.

Chapter 4

94. Fairfax County Land DB: 14, p. 429.
95. Fairfax County Minute Book: 1880, p. 188, submitted November 17, 1887.
96. Fairfax County Minute Book 14, p. 116.

Part II

Chapter 1

97. Constance K. Ring, "Richard Ratcliffe: The Man, His Courthouse, and His Town," in *Yearbook: Historical Society of Fairfax County 1995*, 85–178. Estate map on p. 98.
98. Ibid., 85–178.
99. Ibid.
100. William Page Johnson II, "Richard Radcliffe: The Founder," *Fare Facs Gazette* 3, no. 1 (Winter 2005): 1–5, http://www.historicfairfax.org/wp-content/uploads/2012/05/HFCI31-2005.pdf.
101. Trexler, *Early African Americans*, 7.
102. Ibid., 30.
103. Ibid., 34.
104. "Jermantown Cemetery | 2021 Wreath-Laying & Remembrance," Jermantown Cemetery Preservation Society, YouTube video, posted January 1, 2022, https://youtu.be/KgfgWFFbKPU.

105. Coracle, www.inthecoracle.org.

106. W.E.A. Van Beek, *Dogon: Africa's People of the Cliffs* (Abrams, 2001), 129.

107. Sarah Kohrs, "Down by the Riverside: Burial Practices of the Enslaved," Coracle, March 1, 2021, https://inthecoracle.org/2021/03/down-by-the-riverside-burial-practices-of-the-enslaved/.

108. J.W. Blassingame, *Slave Testimony: Two Centuries of Letters, Speeches, Interviews, and Autobiographies* (Louisiana State University, 1977), 650.

109. Virginia, U.S., Compiled Census and Census Substitutes Index, 1607–1890, 18, Ancestry.com.

110. Ross Netherton and Ruby Waldeck, *The Fairfax Courthouse* (Fairfax, VA: Fairfax County Office of Comprehensive Planning, 1977), 13.

111. Fairfax County, Record of Surveys, 1742–1856, 93.

112. City of Fairfax charter, Legislative Information System, Commonwealth of Virginia, https://law.lis.virginia.gov/charters/fairfax/.

113. Robison, "Little River Turnpike."

114. Ibid.

115. Ring, "Richard Ratcliffe," 85–178.

116. Fairfax Court Order Book 1802, p. 12, FCCHRC.

117. Robison, "Little River Turnpike."

118. "Little River Turnpike," Story of Ravensworth, http://ravensworthstory.org/landmarks/little-river-turnpike/.

119. Robison, "Little River Turnpike."

120. "Notice," *Alexandria Daily Advertiser*, January 19, 1808.

121. Robison, "Little River Turnpike."

122. Ibid.

123. "Little River Turnpike," Story of Ravensworth.

124. Ring, "Richard Ratcliffe," 85–178.

125. 1820 United States Federal Census; Truro Parish, Fairfax, Virginia, for Richard Ratcliffe and enslaved, p. 8.

126. March 29, 1815, Fairfax Will Book P-0, p. 57, FCCHRC.

127. An Inventory and Appraisement of the Personal Estates of Richard Ratcliffe (initially assessed June 22, 1826), February 15, 1830, Fairfax Will Book P-1, p. 395–97, FCCHRC.

128. Fairfax Will Book P-1, p. 395, FCCHRC.

129. Rumsey purchased a portion of Ratcliff's Mount Vineyard from T.R. Love in 1842, per the Fairfax Circuit Court DB G-3, p. 274–75, FCCHRC.

130. Email exchange with Tony Zipfel, Truro Anglican Church patron, 2022.

131. Edward Coleman Trexler Jr., *Anglican Churches, Fairfax Court House, Virginia: 1607–2021* (James River Valley, 2013), 38.

132. William Page Johnson II, "Coombs Cottage," *Fare Facs Gazette* 8, no. 1 (Winter 2005): http://www.historicfairfax.org/wp-content/uploads/2012/05/HFCI31-2005.pdf.

133. Trexler, *Anglican Churches*, 38.

134. Rumsey sells to Maria and Samuel T. Brown in 1856, Fairfax Circuit Court DB X-3, p. 373–75.

135. In Chancery case *Rumsey vs. Brown*, the land was returned to Rumsey in 1867. DB H-4, p. 202, FCCHRC.

136. Ibid.

137. Ibid.

138. "Ox Hill Battlefield Park," Official Site of Fairfax County, https://www.fairfaxcounty.gov/parks/ox-hill.

139. Trexler, *Early African Americans*, 36.

140. Ibid.

141. Edward T. Wenzel, *Chronology of the Civil War in Fairfax County Part One* (Bull Run Civil War Round Table, 2015), 153.

142. "Fairfax City Cemetery," Find a Grave, https://www.findagrave.com/cemetery/50180/Fairfax-City-Cemetery.

143. Sutphin, *Nothing Remains the Same*, 38.

144. Fairfax County, Virginia, Will Book C2:180, Inventory & Appraisement of William Henry Fitzhugh. 1830; Fairfax Circuit Court Historic Records Center, Fairfax, Virginia.

Chapter 2

145. Trexler, *Early African Americans*, 34.

146. Sutphin, *Nothing Remains the Same*, 18.

147. Edward Trexler Jr., "Changing Hands, Fairfax Court House," *Fare Facs Gazette* 9, no. 3 (Summer 2012): 8, https://www.historicfairfax.org/wp-content/uploads/2012/05/HFCI93-2012.pdf.

148. *Long Island Farmer and Advertiser*, July 23, 1861.

149. Trexler Jr., "Changing Hands."

150. Sutphin, *Nothing Remains the Same*, 41.

151. Trexler Jr., "Changing Hands."

152. Fairfax City walking tour notes collected by Jenee Lindner.

153. Sutphin, *Nothing Remains the Same*, 1.

154. Trexler Jr., "Changing Hands."
155. Sutphin, *Nothing Remains the Same*, 41–42.
156. Ibid., 18–19.
157. Rita Colbert, descendant phone conversation, April 2022.
158. Kamp Washington, Fairfax, Virginia—George Mason University Archival Repository, "The Randolph H. Lytton Historical Postcards of Fairfax, Virginia Collection," http://mars.gmu.edu/handle/1920/5111.
159. Discussion with Rita Colbert and author.
160. Sutphin, *Nothing Remains the Same*, 40.
161. Ibid., 40–42.
162. Told to author by Etta Willson, longtime resident of the area, May 2022.

Chapter 3

163. William Page Johnson II, "The Race Field at Fairfax Court House," *Fare Facs Gazette* 13, no. 2 (Spring 2016), https://www.historicfairfax.org/wp-content/uploads/2016/08/HFCI1302-2016.pdf.
164. Author discussions with descendant Rita Colbert, March 2022.
165. Trexler, *Early African Americans*, 75.
166. Facebook post, July 2022.
167. Trexler, *Early African Americans*, 39.
168. Ibid., 83.
169. Mt. Calvary Baptist Church, https://mtcalvaryfairfax.net/.
170. Ibid.
171. William Page Johnson II, personal correspondence with Etta Bowles Richards Strozier, January 31, 2006.
172. William Page Johnson II, "African American Education in the Town/City of Fairfax," *Fare Facs Gazette* 4, no. 1 (Winter 2006), https://www.historicfairfax.org/wp-content/uploads/2012/05/HFCI41-2006.pdf.
173. "Retired Teacher, Now 98, Recalls Lunch Pails, Slate Boards," *Fairfax County Public Schools Bulletin* 6, no. 10 (June 1970).
174. Obituary of Minnie B. Hughes, *Martinsville Bulletin*, September 30, 1975.
175. William Page Johnson II, "The Freedmen's Bureau and School at Fairfax Courthouse," *Fare Facs Gazette* 13, no. 4 (2016), https://www.historicfairfax.org/wp-content/uploads/2012/05/HFCI1304-2016.pdf;

"Extracts from the Second Annual Report of Friends' Association of Phila. for the Aid and Elevation of the Freedmen," *Friends Intelligencer* 23, no. 16 (June 23, 1866), 249–52.

176. Page Johnson II, "Freedmen's Bureau and School."

177. Ibid.

178. Ibid.

179. Ibid.

180. "The Rosenwald Schools: Progressive Era Philanthropy in the Segregated South," Teaching with Historic Places, U.S. National Park Service, U.S. Department of the Interior.

181. "March Meeting of the School Board," *News-Observer*, March 12, 1925, https://virginiachronicle.com.

182. William Page Johnson II, personal correspondence with Mabel Payne Colbert, February 10, 2006.

183. William Page Johnson II, personal communication with Warren Hunter, February 16, 2006.

184. "School History: Fairfax Elementary School," School History: Fairfax Elementary School, Fairfax County Public School System.

185. "Brown v. Board of Education," History, October 27, 2009, https://www.history.com/topics/black-history/brown-v-board-of-education-of-topeka.

186. *Fairfax County: A History*, 578.

187. Virginius Dabney, *Virginia: The New Dominion* (Garden City, NJ: Doubleday, 1971), 531.

188. *Fairfax County: A History*, 579.

189. Ibid., 580.

190. Robbins L. Gates, *The Making of Massive Resistance* (Chapel Hill: University of North Carolina Press, 1964), 145–47.

191. *Fairfax County Sun-Echo*, March 1957; *Congressional Christian Church of Fairfax County Newsletter* (February 13, 1957).

192. *Fairfax County: A History*, 581.

193. William Page Johnson II, "African American Education in the Town/City of Fairfax," *Fare Facs Gazette* 4, no. 1 (Winter 2006), https://www.historicfairfax.org/wp-content/uploads/2012/05/HFCI41-2006.pdf.

194. Ibid.

195. Viola Orr was the widow of Richard R. Farr III, Wilson Farr's brother: Farr Land Chain. Fairfax Circuit Court Historic Records, Fairfax County, Virginia.

196. "City History," City of Fairfax Virginia.

197. George Mason University: Center for Mason Legacies—Black Lives Next Door, John C. Wood Papers, "Example Acquisitions Notice," 1968. Researcher: Sydney Alexandria Hardy.
198. DeNeen L. Brown, "A Bit of Va. History is On the Block: Developer Makes Bid for Last Black Enclave in Fairfax City," *Washington Post*, August 14, 1989, https://www.washingtonpost.com/archive/local/1989/08/14/a-bit-of-va-history-is-on-the-block/68a6ce74-ff6f-4798-81be-3837c0c5247c/.
199. Information obtained from descendants to Jenee Lindner in 2023.
200. Jenee Lindner, discussions with Etta Willson, Rita Colbert, Rondia Prescott and Jerry McMillian, all former residents, September 2023.
201. Fairfax City Community Development and Planning database, Fairfax, Virginia; Jenee Lindner, researcher; August 29, 2023.

PART III

Chapter 1

202. U.S. Census of 1870, Providence, Fairfax County, Virginia.
203. *Alexandria Gazette*, December 8, 1866.
204. *Boston Herald*, May 30, 1897.
205. *Fairfax News*, December 14, 1872.
206. *Alexandria Gazette*, January 3, 1874.
207. *Tampa Tribune*, December 31, 1918. John Lee McWhorter was the associate editor of the *Tampa Tribune* in 1918. He was born at Fairfax Court House in 1867, the son of Dr. William and Mary (Millan) McWhorter. He died in Alexandria, Virginia, in 1928.
208. Ross D. Netherton and Ruby Waldeck, *The Fairfax County Courthouse* (Fairfax, VA: Fairfax County Office of Comprehensive Planning, 1977), 1.
209. *Dewey v. Ferguson*, (1890), Fairfax County Chancery Suit.
210. Fairfax County DB K5, p. 88, January 31, 1891.
211. *Alexandria Gazette*, March 21, 1890.
212. *Evening Star*, November 12, 1892.
213. Fairfax County DB A6, p. 383, March 14, 1898.
214. *Alexandria Gazette*, April 5, 1898.
215. George H. Carroll (1857–1903) was formerly enslaved by Harrison and Narcissa Monroe. He was married to Alice Virginia Chapman (185–1916) in April 1882 in Washington, D.C. George H. Carroll

purchased the same portion of lot no. 15 from the estate of Narcissa Monroe in 1886, which he, in turn, sold to Susan Ferguson in 1899. George H. Carroll was born on November 1857. He died on February 4, 1903, in Washington, D.C. (see *Evening Star*, February 9, 1903). His funeral took place from Ebenezer M.E. Church, cor. Fourth and D Streets SE. George and Alice are believed to be buried in Mount Zion Cemetery in Washington, D.C. Daughter, Annie Carroll, born February 1882.

216. Fairfax County DB D6, p. 276, September 12, 1899, FCCHRC.

217. The 1870 census of Fairfax County, Virginia, enumerates Narcissa Monroe, White; Susan Carroll, age twenty-nine, Black; and George Carroll, age twelve, Black—both domestic servants. Slave Census of 1860, Fairfax County, enumerates two slaves owned by Narcissa Monroe: a Black female, age eighteen, and a Black male, age two; accessed via Ancestry.com.

218. Fairfax County DB O5, p. 623, June 22, 1893, FCCHRC.

219. *Campbell v. Ferguson*, (1903), Fairfax County Chancery Suit.

220. *Fairfax Herald*, July 2, 1886, and August 21, 1903; *Commonwealth of Virginia v. James Ferguson*, September 1886 term. Indictment for Selling Liquor w/o a License, Ffx. Co. Cir. Ct. Clk.

221. *Fairfax Herald*, March 22, 1901.

222. The law firm Moore and Keith was composed of partners Robert Walton Moore (1859–1941) and Thomas Randolph Keith (1872–1937).

223. *Campbell v. Ferguson* (1903), letter to George Carroll by persons unknown, Fairfax County Chancery Suit.

224. *Washington Bee*, July 2, 1887.

225. *Campbell v. Ferguson* (1903), Fairfax County Chancery Suit.

226. Ibid.

227. Census of 1920, Manhattan, New York.

Chapter 2

228. "Colored Grand Jury," *Fairfax Herald*, vol. 54, no. 1, p. 4. May 31, 1935. *Library of Virginia, Virginia Chronicles*. Richmond, Virginia. "African American Jurors," Fairfax County African American History Inventory. Fairfax County Circuit Court Historic Records Center. "Colored Men Drawn on Current Court Trial Jury List." *Fairfax Herald*, vol. 54, no. 25, p. 1. November 22, 1935. *Library of Virginia, Virginia Chronicles*. Richmond, Virginia.

229. Fairfax County Colored Citizens Association Anniversary Pamphlet 1928–1941, p. 1, Virginia Room, Fairfax County Public Library.

230. Ibid., 5.

231. Fairfax County Historic Records Center: Fairfax Minute Book 17, p. 70.

232. 1930 U.S. Federal Census.

233. Year: 1940; Census Place: Lee, Fairfax, Virginia; Roll: m-t0627-04261; Page: 1B; Enumeration District: 30-14.

234. "Sideburn Is More Than a Name," Connection Newspapers, June 30, 2004, www.connectionnewspapers.com. Nellie White, a Black woman who lived several years after her husband passed away, managed their 150 acres until developers came to call in 1964. They named Nellie White Lane after her. When sold, there were only five houses in the Sideburn area.

235. U.S. Social Security Applications and Claims Index, 1936–2007, Ancestry.com.

236. Board of Supervisor Minute Book No. 5, p. 432, and from Nan Netherton et al., *Fairfax County, Virginia: A History* (Fairfax, VA: Fairfax County Board of Supervisors: 1978), 611.

237. Email exchange with the Burke, Virginia author and historian Corazon Foley, June 2, 2023.

238. Year: 1940; Census Place: Fairfax, Fairfax, Virginia; Roll: m-t0627-04261; Page: 3B; Enumeration District: 30-23.

239. United States of America, Bureau of the Census; Washington, D.C.; Seventeenth Census of the United States, 1950; Record Group: Records of the Bureau of the Census, 1790–2007; Record Group Number: 29; Residence Date: 1950; Home in 1950: Fairfax, Fairfax, Virginia; Roll: 3020; Sheet Number: 30; Enumeration District: 30-58.

240. Year: 1920; Census Place: Falls Church, Fairfax, Virginia; Roll: T625_1886; Page: 12B; Enumeration District: 33.

241. Year: 1930; Census Place: Falls Church, Fairfax, Virginia; Page: 9B; Enumeration District: 0009; FHL microfilm: 2342176.

242. *News-Observer*, November 9, 1939.

243. Year: 1940; Census Place: Falls Church, Fairfax, Virginia; Roll: m-t0627-04261; Page: 12B; Enumeration District: 30-9.

244. *Evening Star*, July 14, 1940.

245. Netherton et al., *Fairfax County, Virginia: A History*, 455–58.

246. Badil-Abish, *Shades of Gray*, 85–88.

247. Fairfax County Land Deed of Record, Liber X, No. 6, p. 466. William Collins bought this land from James M. Mason on December 5, 1905. He purchased another two acres in 1912.

248. Marion Dobbins, "Freedmen of Northern Virginia; Independence Through Landownership, Black Communities and the Northern Virginia Baptist Association," written for George Mason University History Course No. 711, 2014, p. 20.

249. Jenee Lindner, discussions with Henry Page's granddaughter Gladys (Woosie) Gaskins, June 2023.

250. Year: 1930; Census Place: Fairfax, Fairfax, Virginia; Page: 4B; Enumeration District: 0021; FHL microfilm: 2342176.

251. Year: *1940*; Census Place: *Fairfax, Fairfax, Virginia*; Roll: *m-t0627-04261*; Page: *3A*; Enumeration District: *30-23*.

252. Tinner Hill Heritage Site, https://www.tinnerhill.org/.

253. Ibid.

254. Andrew M.D. Wolf, *Black Settlement in Fairfax County, Virginia during Reconstruction* (Fairfax, VA: Fairfax County Office of Comprehensive Planning, 1975), 41.

255. Ibid.

256. *Evening Star* (Washington, D.C.), June 24, 1919.

257. Year: 1940; Census Place: Falls Church, Fairfax, Virginia; Roll: m-t0627-04261; Page: 26A; Enumeration District: 30-9.

258. Netherton et al., *Fairfax County, Virginia*, 577.

259. Appeared in the *Washington Post*, September 29, 1964; Find a Grave, Memorial No. 70280481.

Chapter 3

260. Prichard/Moore/Donahoe/McCandlish family, *Remembering Our Grandmother* (privately printed, 2020).

261. Lynwood Payne, speaking by phone to the author, April 2022.

262. Discussions between Jenee Lindner and Tom Prichard with review of interview notes. November 2022.

263. Mathelle K. Lee, *A History of Luther P. Jackson High School: A Report of a Case Study on the Development of a Black High School* (PhD diss. submitted to the Faculty of Virginia Polytechnic Institute, School of Education, 1993), https://vtechworks.lib.vt.edu.

264. Antoinette G. van Zelm, "Dean, Jennie Serepta (1848–1913)," Virginia Foundation for the Humanities, www.encyclopediavirginia.org.

265. Frank Mustac, "Two Families Reflect Two Histories: Long Bloodlines Weave Road to Fairfax City's Past, Future," *Fairfax Times Community News*, February 24, 2005.

266. Ibid.

267. van Zelm, "Dean, Jennie Serepta."

268. Lee, *Luther P. Jackson High School*.

269. Jaya Patil, "The Legacy of an Archivist," *Fairfax County Times*, March 25, 2022, https://www.fairfaxtimes.com/articles/fairfax_county/the-legacy-of-an-archivist/article_ee0c2cac-aba6-11ec-b4e0-97e5553f6aa2.html.

270. E-mail from John "Chap" Petersen to Jenee Lindner, June 2023.

271. Patil, "Legacy of an Archivist."

272. William Page Johnson II, "My Ten Favorite People in Fairfax Cemetery: Lieut. Edgar Allen Prichard (1920–2000)," *Fare Facs Gazette* (Fall 2005), https://www.historicfairfax.org/wp-content/uploads/2012/05/HFCI34-2005.pdf.

273. Discussions between Jenee Lindner and Tom Prichard with review of interview notes. Feb. 2023

274. Edgar Prichard, *Settling in Fairfax*, vol. 4 of *Autobiography of a Broken-Down County Lawyer* (self-published, 2000), 263.

275. Discussions between Jenee Lindner and Tom Prichard with review of interview notes. Feb. 2023

276. "School History," Fairfax County Public Schools, https://jacksonms.fcps.edu/about/history.

277. Prichard et al., *Remembering Our Grandmother*.

Chapter 4

278. Robert W. Prichard, PhD, is an emeritus professor of church history at the Virginia Theological Seminary in Alexandria.

279. Alison Bauer Campbell, "The Road to Integration: Arlington Public Schools 1959–1971," *Arlington Historical Magazine* (October 1996), 27–42, 1996-4-Integration.pdf (arlingtonhistoricalsociety.org).

280. "Desegregation Reports," Fairfax County Public Schools, https://www.fcps.edu/about-fcps/history/records/desegregation/reports.

281. Although E.A. Prichard graduated from the University of Virginia Law School and settled and spent the rest of his life in Fairfax (his wife's hometown), he had spent his early years in Brockton, Montana, a small railroad town located on the Fort Peck Indian Reservation. See Edgar Allen Prichard, *Growing Up in Montana*, vol. 1 of *Autobiography of a Broken Down Country Lawyer* (Fairfax, VA: privately printed, 1995), 80.

282. Louise P. Engle, "Brotherhood Week Observed by N.C.C.J.: Francis Pickens Miller Will Give Principal Address," *Fairfax Standard*, February 15, 1952.

283. The members of the Thompson Committee asked David Scull to answer a series of thirty-one questions about supporters of integration. The twentieth question was: "Has Mr. E. A. Prichard used [mailbox number 218 in Annandale, which was the return address used in mailings of publicity in the support of integration]?" See Law Legal News, U.S. Supreme Court, *Scull v. Virginia*, 359 U.S. 344 (1959), 359 U.S. 344 (argued November 18, 1958, decided May 4, 1959), http://news.findlaw.com.

284. "Fairfax Church Is Told to Evict CORE Institute," *Washington Post*, August 24, 1961.

285. The poll tax was a per-person voting tax adopted as part of the Virginia Constitution of 1902 to prevent voting by poor Blacks and Whites. In order to qualify to vote, residents otherwise qualified to vote needed to pay a tax of $1.50 for the three years prior to the election in which they hoped to vote. The tax levied in 1902 is the equivalent of $52.91 in 2023 dollars. For Nancy M. McCandlish's opposition to the tax, see "Virginia Poll Tax Is Assailed as 'Mockery,'" *Washington Post*, July 5, 1941.

286. There were also rumors passed among high school students at the time that Mr. Smith purchased and resold alcohol to minors, something that George Mason officials did not want to happen to their students.

287. "New Negro City Councilmen Signal a Changing Virginia," *Washington Post*, June 20, 1968.

PART IV

Chapter 1

288. William E. Montgomery, *Under Their Own Vine and Fig Tree: The African-American Church in the South 1865–1900* (Louisiana State University Press, 1993), 127.

289. Montgomery, *Vine and Fig Tree*, 111.

290. Ibid., 99.

291. Eric Foner, *Reconstruction: America's Unfinished Revolution: 1863–1877* (HarperCollins, 1988).

292. Netherton et al., *Fairfax County, Virginia*, 450.

293. Ibid.

294. Ibid., 452.

295. Ibid.

296. Ibid.

297. "Odrick's Corner Located with Historic Marker," *Fairfax Connection*, May 20, 2002.

298. President Jimmy Carter to Northern Virginia Baptist Association, August 22, 1977.

299. *First Baptist Church of Warrenton: One Hundred Year Anniversary* (Warrenton, VA, 1967).

300. Fourteenth Annual Northern Virginia Baptist Association Session Minutes, Pleasant Grove Baptist Church, Orange County, Virginia, August 19–21, 1891, accessed from the Afro American Museum, Plains, Virginia.

301. Seventy-Fifth Annual Northern Virginia Baptist Association Session Minutes, August 1952, accessed from the Afro-American Museum, Plains, Virginia.

302. Fourteenth Annual Northern Virginia Baptist Association Session Minutes. The total membership listed in this minute book was 346 for First Baptist of Warrenton—more than any other church assembled with the NVBA.

303. Stephen Johnson Lewis, *Undaunted Faith; The Story of Jennie Dean* (Manassas Museum System, 1994), 5.

304. Seventy-Fifth Annual Northern Virginia Baptist Association Session Minutes.

305. Ibid.

306. "Some Eventful Thoughts," Northern Virginia Baptist Association, 1967.

307. Fourteenth Annual Northern Virginia Baptist Association Session Minutes.

308. Ibid.

309. Montgomery, *Vine and Fig Tree*, 111.

Chapter 2

310. Nan Netherton and Whitney Von Lake Wyckoff, *Fairfax Station: All Aboard!* (Fairfax, VA: Friends of the Fairfax Station, 1995), 20; City of Fairfax Virginia, "City History," https://www.fairfaxva.gov/government/historic-resources/city-history.

311. *John Morarity v. Robert Allison, admr.*, 1867, Term Papers Box 076 TP 1869-214 to TP 1869-319; *Chancery Cases: Johnathan Roberts (Sheriff) Admr. of Robert Allison v. Martha A. Allison, Widow & Heirs of James G. Allison,*

1879, CFF 2N p. 2 or 2, Fairfax County Courthouse Historic Records Center, hereafter FCCHRC.

312. The 1870 and 1880 U.S. Census list their children; John identifies the children as products of his relationship with Eliza in his will, Will Book 2, p. 470, 1900, FCCHRC.

313. U.S. Census Bureau 1880, retrieved from www.ancestry.com; Death Register cards for Eliza Morarity and Eliza Turley, FFCCHR; *Register of Deaths, Fairfax County, Providence Township*, for the year ending December 31, 1874, and again in *Register of Deaths, Fairfax County, Southern District*, for the year ending December 31, 1875, FFCCHR. It is unclear why the death was reported in two different years, in two districts, but it is safe to assume that this is the same person.

314. DB I-5 p. 69, FFCCHR.

315. *General Register, Fairfax County, 1902–1903*, "Roll of White Voters Registered at F(airfax)C(ourt)H(ouse)," FFCCHR; Trexler, *Early African Americans*, 68.

316. Marriage license for Thomas Morarity and Venie Gibson, November 14, 1896, Fairfax County, retrieved from Ancestry.com; for a discussion on the culture surrounding "passing" in the late nineteenth century, see Carl Jacoby, *The Strange Career of William Ellis, The Texas Slave Who Became a Mexican Millionaire* (New York: Norton, 2016).

317. DB 666 p 291, FCCHRC.

318. DB J-5, p. 524, FCCHRC.

319. DB 1025, p. 84, FCCHRC.

320. "John Morarity Obituary," *Fairfax Herald*, February 26, 1904, 3.

321. Anne Dobberteen, "The Immigrant: John Morarity," George Mason University: Center for Mason Legacies—Black Lives Next Door, 2022, https://legacies.gmu.edu/research/black-lives-next-door.

Chapter 3

322. DB C-7, p. 136, FCCHRC.

323. "Death of J. S. Barbour—Dean of Fairfax Bar Passes Away, Tuesday Morning Last, Following Long Illness," *Fairfax Herald*, May 9, 1952.

324. Susan Breitzer, "Constitutional Convention, Virginia (1901–1902)," *Encyclopedia Virginia*, Virginia Humanities, March 23, 2021, https://encyclopediavirginia.org/entries/constitutional-convention-virginia-1901-1902/.

325. DB O-7, p. 416 and Deed Book P R-7, p. 545, FCCHRC.
326. DB Q-8, p. 607, FCCHRC.
327. DB F-8, p. 461, FCCHRC.
328. DB R-8, p.366, FCCHRC.
329. DB R-8, p.491, FCCHRC.
330. DB W-8, p.61, FCCHRC.
331. DB A-9 p. 209, FCCHRC; for more on the deleterious impacts of *Plessy v. Ferguson*, see Blair Murphy Kelley, *Right to Ride: Streetcar Boycotts and African American Citizenship in the Era of Plessy v. Ferguson* (Chapel Hill: University of North Carolina Press, 2010).
332. DB 729 p. 65, FCCHRC; Mt. Calvary Baptist Church, "History," https://mtcalvaryfairfax.net/about-us/.
333. See also Paige Glotzer, *How the Suburbs Were Segregated: Developers and the Business of Exclusionary Housing, 1890–1960* (New York: Columbia University Press, 2020). Glotzer's work examines how the real estate industry shaped residential segregation in Baltimore during the same period.
334. See also Richard Rothstein, *The Color of Law: A Forgotten History of How Our Government Segregated America* (New York: Liveright, 2017).
335. Anne Dobberteen, "The Segregationist Dairy Farmer: John S. Barbour," 2022, George Mason University: Center for Mason Legacies—Black Lives Next Door, https://legacies.gmu.edu/research/black-lives-next-door.

Chapter 4

336. The *1902–1903 Roll of Colored Voters Registered at Fairfax CH Precinct in Providence* lists Horace Gibson as a blacksmith in Ilda. Strother Gibson is listed as a farmer in Fairfax Courthouse. John Groomes (Bradshaw's father) was listed as a farmer in Fairfax Courthouse, at Fairfax County Historic Courthouse; *Luvenia Morarity vs. Martha Groomes*, administratrix of Strother Gibson, et al; Chancery Court of Fairfax County, 1937; case files accessible through FCCHRC; see CPI Inflation Calculator website for monetary conversion, https://www.in2013dollars.com/us/inflation/1927?amount=536.78; Badil-Abish, *Shades of Gray*, 40–42.
337. DB M-6 p. 81, FCCHRC; Venie Gibson and Thomas Morarity Marriage Certificate, 1896, Fairfax County Courthouse; "Thank You Notice," *Fairfax Herald*, November 27, 1931; "Mrs. Louvenia Morarity Obituary," *Fairfax Herald*, July 22, 1949.

338. DB T-10 p. 474–77, FCCHRC.

339. U.S. Census Bureau 1920; *Washington, D.C., U.S., Marriage Records, 1810–1953*, retrieved through Ancestry.com.

340. DB W-8 p. 61, DB E-10, p. 119, DB 657, p. 256, FCCHRC.

341. "Louis Morarity Mt. Calvary Baptist Ch. Clerk," *Fairfax Herald*, July 17, 1964, 1; Lester Page's nephew, Clarence Page Jr., remembered his uncle's plumbing business in a conversation in March 2022.

342. Martha G. Groomes owned her own lot, lot 16 in the original plat, and then lots 38 and 39 on the 1962 tax maps, within her husband Bradshaw's subdivision on the west side of Rt. 123 (labeled in DB L-9 p. 31, recorded in DB X-12 p. 126-7, FCCHRC). Her father, Strother, built a house on her lot that she had planned to subdivide and sell to him, but he died before he could purchase the land on which he had built a home for himself on Rt. 123. The land was eventually sold to the Allen family to settle Strother's estate in 1936 (DBB-12 p 339–44, FCCHRC), and Martha maintained her home on 123 until her death.

343. *Washington, D.C., U.S., Compiled Marriage Index, 1830–1921*, retrieved from Ancestry.com; *U.S. Census Bureau* 1940, Ancestry.com; "Bradshaw Groomes Gives Large Outing Picnic," *Fairfax Herald*, September 11, 1914.

344. "Groomes Bradshaw Adv. Hogs for sale," *Fairfax Herald*, December 8, 1939; "Groomes Brad Arrested for Illegal Liquor Sales," *Fairfax Herald*, August 19, 1938; Martha and Bradshaw Groomes divorce lawsuit deposition and file, case no. 6000, 1943, available through FCCHRC. Even after the divorce went through, Martha repeatedly asked the court to intervene to extricate Brad from the home that she owned.

345. DB 417 p. 59; DB 7860, p. 925, FCCHRC.

346. Sydney-Alexandria Hardy, "'Back to School' Next to Our University: The History of a Long-Standing Black Community in Fairfax," https://research.centerformasonslegacies.com/s/blnd/page/-back-to-school-an-in-depth-look-at-the-forgotten-historic-location.

347. Anne Dobberteen, "Family Connections: Matrilineal Roots of the School Street Community," George Mason University: Center for Mason Legacies—Black Lives Next Door, 2022, https://legacies.gmu.edu/research/black-lives-next-door.

PART V

Chapter 1

348. David Quimette extrapolated these numbers, based on Angus Maddison, *The World Economy: A Millennial Perspective* (2001), 241, table B-10. Taken from an Elder Gerrit Gong conference talk, "We Each Have a Story," April 2022, the Church of Jesus Christ of Latter-day Saints.

INDEX

R

S

ABOUT THE AUTHORS

Etta Willson is a longtime genealogist and poetic writer about her family and her ancestors.

Rita Colbert is the Fairfax City Black community photo acquisitions coordinator, receiving photo albums after friends and family pass away.

Rondia Prescott is vice president of the Jermantown Cemetery Preservation Society and Fairfax County (SACC) substitute staff supervisor/coordinator.
    All three—Willson, Colbert and Prescott—were longtime residents of the Black Fairfax City communities now gone.

Linneall Naylor, president of the Jermantown Cemetery Preservation Society and FCPS teacher, was raised in D.C. but returned to find her roots. She is a well-regarded family history speaker.

Jenee Lindner is a Fairfax County history commissioner and a longtime resident of Fairfax County, and she gives Fairfax City/County historical lectures. She has a master's degree from Stanford University in education and history. She has also found family roots in these communities.